Writing Television Drama

Nicholas Gibbs

Hodder Education

338 Euston Road, London NW1 3BH.

Hodder Education is an Hachette UK company

First published in UK 2012 by Hodder Education

First published in US 2012 by The McGraw-Hill Companies, Inc.

Copyright © 2012 Nicholas Gibbs

Writing Television

Nicholas Gibbs

*This book is dedicated to my fellow writers
Natalie Cheary, Paul Fleming and Carol Kearney.*

*It is also dedicated to my family, Gaynor, Stevanie and
Skye.*

*And finally it is dedicated to all those writers who
write or want to write television drama.*

Acknowledgements and credits

First I would like to thank everyone in the television drama industry who advised me and provided me with information during the writing of this book including Paul Ashton (BBC Writersroom), Caryl Benee (ITV), Laura Brown (BBC), Natalie Cheary, Rachelle Constant (BBC), Victoria Fea (ITV), Amy Gill (Red Productions), Eleanor Goldwin (BBC), Simon Harper (BBC/*Holby City*), Lucy Hay (Bang2write), Estelle Hind (ITV), Lisa Holdsworth, Francis Hopkinson (ITV Studios), Charlotte Jones, Tony Jordan (Red Planet), Bryan Kirkwood, Nicola Larder, Beth Levison (BBC), Hayley McKenzie, Marc Pye, Lisa Regan (Lime Pictures), Jenny Robins, Leah Schmidt, Emma Smithwick (Lime Pictures), Ben Stephenson (BBC), Ben Stoll (Channel 4), Sally Wainwright and Kirsten Wardlaw (ITV), plus the many more who have chipped in and helped facilitate research and interviews.

The author and publisher would like to thank the following companies for permission to print the following extracts:

Figure 6.1: From the pilot episode of *Harry's Law* © Bonanza Productions Inc.

Figure 7.1: From *Hustle*, Series 1, Episode 1 © Kudos Film and Television

Figures 10.1 and 10.2: From 'The Flasher', episode *of The Street* © ITV Granada

Figure 10.3: From 'The Socrates Method', episode of *House* © Universal Television

Figure 10.4: From *Hustle*, Series 1, Episode 1 © Kudos Film and TV

Figures 11.1, 11.2 and 11.3: From 'Left Field', episode of *New Tricks* © Wall to Wall

Contents

Meet the author

Welcome to *Writing Television Drama*!

Fellow writers, I have felt your pain and your frustration. I have experienced script readers read the same script where one has praised and loved the beautifully executed characterization and another has said the characterization wasn't rounded enough! I have been long-listed, short-listed, not even listed (for the same piece of work). I have had scripts championed by producers. I have had projects miss out through timing, budgets and the very system itself! So has every credited writer whose work ends up on screen.

I am a writer and BBC-trained script editor who is asked to read and provide feedback for scripts. I get asked to run scriptwriting workshops and do the occasional lecture on the subject. I love stories and always have done – from writing my very first tale about astronauts meeting dragons on the Moon at the age of six to my more recent forays into journalism, theatre and radio. My first love, though, is television drama and the people who want to and do make it.

I hope this book is useful to you, the writer.

Nicholas Gibbs

May 2012

Introduction

Everyone loves stories. Everyone loves stories told on television – from the wonder of the childhood years through the rebellious teen stories to the 'big themes' as the world opens up to adulthood. These are stories that tell us about lives beyond the walls of our home, our street, our town, our nation, our planet, our time or even our universe.

All stories, all dramas, tell us something about the human condition. About what man was, what man is, what man will be, what man could be. From gritty social dramas such as Jimmy McGovern's *Accused*, to the splendour of Julian Fellowes' *Downtown Abbey*, the comic fantasy of Toby Whithouse's *Being Human*, and the intensity of Neil Cross's *Luther*.

We root for the cops and private detectives that seek to solve crime in their own inimitable way from the marvellously reimagined *Sherlock* to the old school of *New Tricks*. We delve into lives of the medical profession in shows such as *Monroe* and *Casualty*.

Casualty, of course, is what the industry terms a 'continuing drama' series. The ultimate continuing drama series is one that has seen more than half a century of stories told about the residents of a little fictitious road in the northern English city of Manchester called *Coronation Street*.

From the United States, we see the cream of American television that elevates the drama bar even higher, with shows such as *House*, about a maverick genius doctor who solves difficult medical cases; *Dexter*, where our hero is a serial killer; *Ugly Betty*, about the girl who dreams of being a writer; and *Battlestar Galactica*, a space opera about mankind in the universe.

These are the shows that have set the bar and with which you, the new upcoming scriptwriter, has to compete – compete with your unique voice, your unique story and your distinctive characters and through a standout good-quality script that has to impress people within the industry.

Aside from the established writers – some of whom are mentioned above – you are also competing against all the other newbie writers. The BBC Writersroom alone receives more than 10,000 speculative scripts a year. The Writers Guild of America registers around 50,000 television and film scripts per year.

This book is designed to help you write the best possible script that you can before you send it off to people within the industry. Within these pages there will be insights from writers as well as interviews with the people you will have to impress with your script – from script readers to commissioners and all points in between. We will reference helpful resources to which you can turn for extra information and advice.

We will also examine the various avenues that are available to get you noticed as a writer – whether you are a novice or someone who has found their ambition stalled. In the second half of the book we will take a snapshot of the industry as it is today and the opportunities available.

There are two elements, however, about which I cannot make any promises, and these are luck and timing. No matter how good your script is, you need both these things. Even established writers need these two elements to coincide for their next project to happen. However, if these two 'gods' do their bit for you, let's make sure that you have your work in the best place it can be.

You do need a completed script and in all probability a second completed script and loads of ideas. An unfinished script is of no help or interest to anyone.

Scriptwriting is not an easy task. What you are aiming to do is to create and present a piece of work of high quality and potential. It will require perseverance and resilience because the road is a tough one. As a minimum, you have got to like your own company and, more importantly, enjoy the actual process of writing. The more you do, the better you will get at it.

Good luck!

> '*Be dedicated, write regularly, see as many films and as much TV as possible and above all finish something.*'
>
> Adrian Hodges, writer (*Primeval, Rome, Survivors*)

1

What is a script?

In this chapter you will learn:
- *how to present a television script*
- *about the basic elements that make up a script on the page*
- *that scriptwriting software can save writers a lot of time.*

To a writer a script is the encapsulation of all their hopes and dreams, something that tells a moving-picture story of wonder, emotion and excitement. Your script is a creative endeavour in which you have made a deep emotional investment and whose passion you hope to convey to others.

For those in the industry, however, a script is an instruction manual. An instruction manual for producers, directors, actors, costume designers, composers and so forth on how to turn your £2.50 worth of printed paper into a multimillion pound/dollar/euro drama for television. Or, in the case of the spec script (aka sample script), something to get you noticed.

Physical elements of a script

So what are the physical elements of a television script? First of all, scripts come in an A4-page layout (width 210mm × length 297mm). The pages of the script are bound together using a Twinlock fastener – which is essentially a two-piece fastener which holds a double hole-punched set of papers together. The fastener is positioned on the left side of the script. These types of fasteners are available from stationery shops.

Font

The industry accepted choice of font for your script is Courier 12 point. On no account use any other font no matter how flashy or pretty the font is. Do not use any point size higher or lower than 12. And please, don't send your script in handwritten. Think about the people who have to read your script. Don't make it hard for them. Later in the production process – if it gets that far – a timing estimate for your script, for each scene and so forth, will need to be made and using Courier 12 point on A4 makes those timings universal.

The script layout: on the page

The script format presented here is a generic one and will be what is expected for your original script. Individual shows (and established writers) have their own script foibles while things such as continuing drama such as *EastEnders* and *Coronation Street* have a different layout for production reasons.

MARGINS

▶ The left margin should be positioned 27mm from the edge of the paper.
▶ The right margin should be positioned 25mm from the edge of the paper.

THE HEADER

The header, which should appear at the top of every page, should include:

▶ your title
▶ the episode title (if applicable)
▶ the page number (at the far right).

For example:

```
THE FADES: Episode One                    1.
```

Or

The header will, of course, also appear as the introductory heading on the first page of your script (see Figure 1.1).

Script elements

The basic elements of the script are:

▶ scene heading
▶ action/description
▶ character
▶ dialogue.

1 SCENE HEADING

The scene heading, also known as a slug line, marks up the start of a new scene and a change in place and/or time of your story. Generally the scene heading, which is written all in capitals, needs to contain three pieces of key information:

1 Whether the scene is an **interior** (INT.) or **exterior** (EXT.) – that is, whether the scene takes place inside or outside.
2 In what **location** the scene takes place. For example:
   ▶ if it is an Exterior, it may be something such as a house or street or car park or forest;
   ▶ if the scene is an Interior, it may take place in a workplace or house or sports club or car.
   If it is inside a particular building you may need to identify a certain room within the building. For example, in a house a scene may take place in the living room, or kitchen, or bedroom. In a workplace it may be in someone's office.
3 The **time of day** – usually depicted simply as DAY or NIGHT. Sometimes the nature of a script may require more specific times, say, if there is a countdown involved or the time of day is important (although this type of specific information can also sometimes be conveyed in the action/description – see below).

Below are two examples of scene headings:

```
EXT. ADAM'S FLAT - DAY

INT. ADAM'S FLAT: KITCHEN - NIGHT
```

There are variations on this, but essentially you want a clear, succinct heading.

2 ACTION/DESCRIPTION

The scene action and scene description are written below the scene heading or between dialogues. It is written in normal (non-capitalized) type, starting at the left margin, and in non-justified paragraphs.

For example:

```
EXT. THE STREET - NIGHT

Brian and Ann walk down the street.
Chris and Stella enter their house on
the other side of the street and wave
goodnight.
```

3 CHARACTER

The character element refers to the name of a character written above each piece of dialogue they speak. The character names are written in capital letters and are positioned 88mm from the left edge of the paper.

4 DIALOGUE

Dialogue is the words that your characters speak. The words are in normal, left-justified type and start 56mm from the edge of the paper written below the character name. In any physical line of dialogue there should be no more than 35 characters (including punctuation and spaces between words) before continuing on the next line.

As with all the elements above no justified text is used. For example:

```
                NICHOLAS

Remember that scriptwriting is fun.

Don't do it if you don't enjoy it.
```

Figure 1.1 shows you how a couple of pages of script should look, though remember the actual script should be A4 size. Look at the BBC Writersroom website or any copy of a script for more examples.

SERIES TITLE

"Episode Title"

<u>TEASER</u>

FADE IN:

EXT. THE CRESSET - DAY

Scene headings (or slug lines) are all written in capitals and
contain three elements: whether the scene is Exterior (EXT.)
or Interior (INT.); where the scene takes place; and when the
scene takes place.

The left margin should be about 27mm (or 12/13 picas) from the
left edge of the page.

The right margin should be about 25mm from the right edge (or
65 picas from the left).

No part of the script has a justified margin setting.

The font for scripts is Courier 12pt.

INT. THE CRESSET: CONFERENCE ROOM - NIGHT

Some interior scenes may need more information - for example a
scene in the Cresset takes place in a certain room.

More action goes here.

                    CHARACTER #1
          A character's name when speaking
          dialogue is in capitals and positioned
          88mm in from the left margin.

                    CHARACTER #2
          Dialogue is not justified but each
          line of dialogue should start at 56mm
          and not go beyond 35 typed characters.

                    CHARACTER #2
          It may be that a scene goes beyond a
          single page.

                    CHARACTER #1
          If it does, then this is how you should
          do the layout by indicating that the
          scene continues on to the next page.

                                              (CONTINUED)

Figure 1.1 Sample pages from a television drama script

```
    SERIES TITLE: "Episode Title"                                    2.

CONTINUED:

                            CHARACTER #1
                  I've started talking...

If scene action interrupts a character's speech on the same
page...

                            CHARACTER #1 (CONT'D)
                  Now I'm talking again.

End the teaser and each act like this.

FADE OUT.

                            END OF TEASER
```

Figure 1.1 (cont.) Sample pages from a television drama script

There are other elements of the script that may be utilized and we will look at them (and how to use them) later in the book. We shall also return to location, action, description, character and dialogue in more detail and how to use them.

It is important to emphasize that your script layout must be correct. Script readers – the first port of call for your spec script – are predisposed to say no, and an incorrect or poor layout could result in your work not even being read. The best recommendation is to purchase scriptwriting software that takes the pain out of the formatting process and allows you to concentrate on the all-important content of your script.

> *'I once worked for an agent who told me to reject any script that wasn't formatted properly. I said that we might be missing a gem. The agent told me: "Don't worry, so will everyone else."'*
>
> Lucy V. Hay, Bang2Write, Script Reader

Electronic scripts

Electronic versions of your script (rather than a hard paper copy) may also sometimes be submitted using industry software such as Final Draft or as a PDF file or Word file. Make sure, however, the script format is adhered to. Final Draft and similar software packages do all the above automatically and save a great deal of time, and so are well worth the investment.

Key advice

▶ Always use 12 point Courier as your font.
▶ Scripts should be printed on A4 paper.
▶ Buy Final Draft or similar scriptwriting software.
▶ Print on one side of the paper only.
▶ Use Twinlock fasteners to bind your script.
▶ Do not use fancy fonts or fancy covers.

2

Television drama formats

In this chapter you will learn:
- *about the main drama formats found on UK and US channels*
- *that writing to fit such formats is not only vital but creatively useful.*

In the UK, television drama is commissioned and broadcast by BBC, ITV, C4, Sky and, albeit rarely, Five. Other broadcasters such as MTV and Nickelodeon are also tentatively beginning to commission domestically produced drama for their British audiences. The BBC, funded by the licence fee, brings drama to the screen across three of its four channels – BBC1, BBC2 and BBC3. There is also children's drama aimed at the under-12s that is shown on CBBC.

TV drama comes under various guises:

▶ A **drama series** is a show that has a regular cast of characters who have episodic adventures but with few or no multi-episode or series story arcs. TV dramas such as *Law and Order*, *Vera* and *New Tricks* fall into this category.

▶ A **drama serial** (or mini-series) is a story that is told over a limited number of episodes with a definite end. Shows such as *Collision*, *Injustice*, *Occupation*, *State of Play* and *The Promise* are prime examples of a drama serial.

▶ A **single play** is a self-contained one-off drama. In recent years the single drama in the UK has manifested itself in biopics such as *Hattie* and *Enid* but also in *United*, *Page Eight* and *Night Watch*. These are the equivalent of the US Movies of the Week.

▶ **Continuing drama** usually refers to dramas that are also described as 'soaps'. These shows are the staples of the television schedule and run all year round and include shows such as *Casualty*, *Doctors*, *EastEnders*, *Holby City* (all BBC), *Coronation Street*, *Emmerdale* (both ITV) and *Hollyoaks* (C4).

BBC drama slots run to 30, 45, 60, 90 and, occasionally, 120 minutes. The 30-minute slots have included the likes of *Bleak House* and *The Nativity*. The 45-minute slot occurs in the early Saturday evening family schedule and has included shows such as *Doctor Who*, *Robin Hood* and *Merlin*. The BBC has also produced weekday afternoon dramas with this running time, including *Land Girls*, *Missing* and *32 Brinkburn Street*.

Most BBC drama is broadcast in one-hour slots either at 8 p.m. or 9 p.m. on BBC1, BBC2 and BBC3 and includes shows such as *Holby City*, *Hustle* and *Being Human*. In terms of pre- 'watershed' drama (before 9 p.m.), *Call the Midwife* and *Waterloo Road* have successfully run from 8.00 p.m. to 9.00 p.m. on BBC1. However, most drama on all channels is for the post-watershed 9 p.m. slot. Feature-length shows that run to 90 minutes or two hours will sometimes be the pilot episode of a new series or event shows.

One-hour dramas dominate the ITV schedules, usually at 9 p.m., with unashamedly populist shows such as *Downton Abbey*,

Whitechapel, *Scott and Bailey*, *Monroe* and *Marchlands*. Some shows such as *Vera* and *Lewis* are two hours long. The reality is that because of advertising breaks and programme sponsorship – the advertising and sponsorship after all pays for the dramas in the first place – the running times are a little different. Table 2.1 illustrates the difference between programme slots and programme running times on the various channels.

ITV has a family of channels with original drama content commissioned by ITV1, ITV2 and CITV. It's a similar story at C4 which also has a family of channels with E4 the other channel that shows original UK scripted content. Five and its family of digital channels run to a similar 'commercial hour' but rarely produce original drama.

Sky's drama hour is modelled on the American TV hour which runs 42/43 minutes. Indeed, the BBC's family 45-minute dramas on a Saturday night, which include *Doctor Who*, *Merlin* and *Robin Hood*,

BBC1 & 2

Time slot	Running time
45 mins	43.00
60 mins	59.00
90 mins	89.00
120 mins	119.00

BBC3

Time slot	Running time
45 mins	43.00
60 mins	57.00

BBC (Daytime)

Time slot	Running time
45 mins	43.00

ITV1 & Channel 4/E4

Time slot	Ad breaks	Running time
30 mins	1	23.00
60 mins	3	46.40
90 mins	4	69.20
120 mins	5	93.30

Table 2.1 Time slots, ad breaks and running times of drama programmes on the major UK television channels

are similar because it is those shows that are expected to have an international market. Sky also produces drama shorts that run for ten minutes and also half-an-hour one-off singles.

In the USA network television and most cable largely runs to a 42/43-minute storytelling slot and usually has four or five acts depending on the show and network. There have been forays into a six-act structure (by ABC) with the first or fifth act split in two.

There are exceptions in the US such as HBO, which, with a subscription-based business model, has no ads and is akin to the BBC hour timings. However, that doesn't mean these channels don't still write to a five-act structure. They do but without the interruption of advertisers and with an eye on the lucrative syndication market.

These timings are important because they may affect the script you write. Which slot is your script best suited for? Which channel? Don't necessarily opt for the commercial stations' shorter versions *because* they are short. It may be that your script would sit better at the BBC or on HBO and, therefore, be better for the longer-form hour.

We will look at structure and storytelling later. However, it is worth stressing here that in television – unlike theatre or cinema – drama must be very structured to fit pre-designated time slots. You have to follow that structure and to fall short is a big sin. On the other hand, the structure of television drama can help you – it should be seen not as imposing creative restraint but as nurturing creative discipline.

Key advice

▶ Scripts must be written to fit a standard TV drama format.
▶ The length of a TV drama can typically vary from half an hour to two hours – most are between 45 and 60 minutes long.
▶ Formats used by commercial channels such as ITV must accommodate commercial breaks and therefore have a ready-made structure.
▶ Writing to suit a format need not be a burden – it can help you to organize your story effectively.

3

....

What is a spec script?

In this chapter you will learn:
- *about the qualities that a script reader looks for in a spec script*
- *about the importance of a daily writing routine and of having a designated writing space.*

A spec script, also known as a 'calling card' script, is an original script that you send to organizations such as the BBC Writersroom, independent production companies, competitions, agents or people within the industry. The primary function of this script is to get you noticed as a scriptwriter. It is highly unlikely, although not impossible, that a spec script will get commissioned.

The spec script should be a demonstration of your ability to be *original*. Original in creating memorable and interesting characters, original in the way you tell your story, original in your dialogue. That spark of originality should leap off the page and arouse the interest of the script reader. It should not be derivative, or a pale imitation, of existing shows. It is all about your unique voice as a writer and your take on the world. A successful spec script could lead you to becoming a commissioned episodic writer or staff writer on another show. This is the reality for the vast majority of scriptwriters – you write an original script as a kind of application to write on other people's shows.

The BBC Writersroom's remit is to look for new and fresh talent. If your script stands out in the slush pile, it could potentially lead to a commission on one of the BBC's continuing dramas such as *Doctors* or *EastEnders* or *Casualty*. It may lead you to becoming represented by an agent who can get your script and future scripts to the people that matter – the producers, executives and commissioners. An independent producer may become your champion as a result of your spec script and that may lead to a commission.

Be original

In the UK, this 'calling card' script must be original. Do not write a script for a past or existing show. No one will be interested in that, and indeed it simply won't be read. Even if your ambition is to write for *Holby City*, do not write a *Holby City* script. The producers of *Holby City*, like everyone else, want original scriptwriters who can create compelling guest characters and stories. If they are interested, the producers may invite you to write a trial script for those shows anyway.

It is worth noting at this point that the US spec script system is a little bit different from the UK one. Although increasingly producers also want to see original work, scriptwriters are encouraged to pitch for the show that they want to write for. They want to know that you know the style and format of the show and are familiar with the characters. However, don't rush off and start work on your brilliant script for your favourite American show – there are certain caveats to be aware of first and we will look at these when we look at the American system later in the book (see Chapter 18). Let's first concentrate on your own original creation.

> *'We want an individual voice. A distinct voice. A writer with something to say and an original, surprising, way of saying it.'*
>
> Paul Ashton, BBC Writersroom

Writing time and space

The first thing I want to encourage you to do is to write every day. This is easy for most professional writers to say as they are getting paid and so can get up each day and write full-time (whatever that actually entails). Most of you, however, probably have other distractions in your day such as your job, your family, your friends and the myriad of other things that call on your time.

Set aside a fixed period of time – around a minimum of 30 minutes each day – to write. Write something – *anything;* just get in to the habit. It may be at the end of the day after the children have gone to bed; it may be before they get up in the morning; it may be on the train or bus as you commute to and from work; it may be in your lunch hour... whenever, wherever, but the key thing is to find the time – it can be done. Talk to the family and say this is what you want to do: Do not disturb! If people know and understand why you need this, in most cases they will be encouraging – they may even bring you a cup of coffee!

Another ideal thing to do at home is have a specific place to write – whether it is a designated room or part of a room where you feel comfortable and relaxed. Decorate the area accordingly so that it is clear it is your writing space. It may be a good idea to have a pin board to which you can affix your ideas for scenes, characters and dialogue written on cards so that you can move them about. Another helpful tip is to decorate the area or part of the wall with images of what you are writing about.

> '*Without the writer, I could do nothing. Ideas can come from all sources, but fundamentally without a writer to turn the idea and the plot into a story, a drama isn't worth making.*'
>
> Nicola Shindler, Producer

Every time you sit there you will know your goal is to write your standout spec script. This is what we are aiming for you to do – write a spec script to get you noticed. To give a little light to brighten the script reader's day and make them want to recommend that someone else higher up the television food chain take a look at it. The standard is high (although there are a great many scripts that are very poor) and you will have to work at it. There will be frustrations, disappointments and you will have to develop a thick skin.

One final piece of advice for this chapter – watch television drama! Learn to understand and appreciate the medium and analyse your favourite shows. Why are they your favourite? By that same token, why *don't* you like other shows? What is wrong with them? Take particular interest in the opening or pilot episodes of shows because that is akin to what you're doing with your original spec script.

Key advice

▶ Look to write an original script, not a script of an existing show
▶ Write every day.
▶ Create a writing space.
▶ Watch television drama.

Industry interview 1: the script reader

Lucy Hay is a script reader and writer who has read for agents and industry organizations. She runs her own script feedback service and online community, Bang2write, for new and experienced writers seeking a critical analysis of their work as well as support. In 2012 she was Associate Producer on the movie Deviation and is also one of the organizers of the annual London Screenwriters' Festival.

Nicholas Gibbs: *How did you start script reading?*

Lucy Hay: I left university with a scriptwriting degree and at that time there was a gap in the market for a low-priced, no-frills script reading service. I was a single mum and I couldn't afford to pay people £75 minimum for a script report. So I thought there must be countless others like me in the same kind of situation who don't have a lot of money to spend who want feedback. I'd already worked for a literary agent so I knew that I could do it. It was something I wanted to do and I saw it as my path into the industry. I was limited in what I could do in terms of paid work in getting into the industry. I had a free rein at the agency and looked at everything. That combined with my degree gave me experience and the cheap price meant I was taken seriously quite quickly.

NG: *Then you started your blog?*

LH: Originally I started the blog as a way to prove to the writers that when I was saying something about their script I was not just saying it for the sake of it. Problems happen with all kinds of scripts, all kinds of movies and all kinds of TV programmes. It goes right across the board; it's not just you. There weren't that many blogs at the time. The only other one was Scriptwriting in the UK which was quite useful for finding out about the craft, and there were all the American ones. So I saw a gap in the market there, too.

NG: *Are there common problems you see in new writers?*

LH: Writers struggle with too much dialogue. They should think about how the scene works and how the dialogue works in that scene.

Otherwise dialogue can run away with you quite quickly. If you want to use ten words, use five. If you want to use five words, use two. If you want to use two, use none. As writers we want to use as many words as possible, but less is more. It's an old cliché but nevertheless it's true.

NG: *What other problems have you seen?*

LH: They don't know who they are writing for and why. Some write solely for the marketplace, in which case it has no soul and no heart. Equally, if you don't write with the marketplace in mind at all, then it can go completely off and nobody knows what you're going on about! Remember who you're writing for – your audience. Lots of people don't know who their audience is, never mind what they want. They don't challenge themselves enough and as a result they don't challenge the audience enough. It's not a question of tick-the-box screenwriting. It's not as simple as that. You can't just have these checklists. You've got to really love your idea, you've got to love your characters and you've got to know why you're doing it.

NG: *Spec scripts are about showing you off as a writer.*

LH: You've got to have that script that proves what you can do, so you can write someone else's idea. It sounds terrible when you say it like that but that is the reality of what happens. I think there are so many television writers who are so in love with their spec that they have lost touch with the reality of the likelihood of it being produced, which is very unlikely. I know writers who have had hundreds of hours on screen and they are no closer to getting their sample script, their dream project, made.

NG: *You've got to enjoy writing and love more than your spec.*

LH: One of the Head Writers on *Coronation Street* said in our session at the London Screenwriters' Festival that it really makes him annoyed when he sees writers trying for various television jobs just because they think it will be an easy access to getting their sample made. It shouldn't be about that. You should go for those television jobs because you love television and you love the idea of writing for this particular channel, this particular show and you believe in it a hundred per cent. Otherwise it is a waste of their time. It is a waste of your time. It is a waste of the audience's time. It is a waste of everyone's time because they are faking it. I can totally see his point. I think a lot of newer screenwriters need to wake up to the fact that a sample is a sample and not necessarily ever going to be made, which is possibly a good thing because in five years from now you're possibly going to look at that sample and go that's not the best that I can do.

NG: *Do you have any advice on handling rejection?*

LH: The only person who stands between you and getting somewhere is you. So if you *want* to fail because 'the producers don't like me' or 'the script readers won't let me through' or 'I didn't get past the first round of a scriptwriting competition', you can find any number of barriers. You just have to dust yourself off and get on with it. Don't go off to your blog and whine about it.

NG: *Do you find writers are too quick to send their work out?*

LH: We live in such an immediate age now with email and such like that people are finishing the script, not letting it settle in their brain, and firing it off straightaway. If it's a spec script or a sample script, there is no time limit even if a producer or agent has said to you that they're interested in reading it at some point. People think: I've got to finish it in the next week or they'll forget about me. What do you think the agent or producer is doing? Are they frantic about not receiving an email from so-and-so writer they just met? No. They have other stuff to get on with and they would prefer to see it at its best and not rushed.

NG: *Do you think writers can sometimes focus on the wrong goal?*

LH: For a long time getting on the BBC Writers' Academy was my goal. I wanted to do that. I had a lot of friends who had got on it or had interviews for it. I felt I was as good as them. I love television and I've literally watched soap opera since I was a child. Why wouldn't they take me? In my arrogance, I thought: Why can't I get on the Writers' Academy? I ended up not getting on for about four years in a row. I went: Right, I've had enough now! So I wrote to Ceri Meyrick who kind of oversaw the application process and said, 'Look, you know that I love soap; you know that I can write; you know I understand the industry; why the hell do I never get past the first round of the Writers' Academy?'

She writes back to me and says: 'We don't doubt that you're passionate, we don't doubt you know your stuff but, to be honest, when we read your stuff, we think films and not TV.' At the time I was really angry but then I realized she was right because all the projects I wanted to be involved in are films. So I asked myself what I was trying to do. I love soap and I'd actually mistaken my love of soap for wanting to do that job because I wanted the money. For me the money was a validation but that is one of the worst reasons for doing any job.

www.bang2write.com

4

....

Preparing the script

In this chapter you will learn:
- *about the importance of having original ideas*
- *what a logline is and how to write one*
- *about what makes a good TV drama title.*

The idea

Any story that you want to write you have to love – you have to want to tell that story because you are going to have to live with it and enthuse about it to other people for a long time. Because you are reading this book, I assume that you *have* ideas – ideas that you think will make great television.

I want you to think about those ideas for a couple of days and write them down. Then go back and look at the list and cross out anything that seems derivative of a recent or existing show. Your spec script needs to stand out, so doing something that is similar to an existing show will just get lost in the mediocre sea of familiar stories.

Hustle creator and writer Tony Jordan received *Hustle*-esque scripts at his production company Red Planet in the wake of its success. Jordan wasn't interested. And why would he be? He was already doing *Hustle*. In the UK, drama producers look for something new and different rather than attempting a poor copy of an existing successful show.

In the US, there is often a feeding frenzy following a breakout hit of a show, as rival broadcasters seek to mimic that success with what they believe to be what the audience wants. However, you are writing an *original* spec script, so the rule still applies of creating a story that nobody else is doing. That is what will get you noticed, and not any pale imitation of a *Dexter* or *Blue Bloods*.

> **'In America Lost, Desperate Housewives and Grey's Anatomy all launched in the same season. All brilliantly original but the next year there were loads of shows that were derivative of them and none of them worked, not a single one worked. So the lesson is move on and be original again.'**
>
> Ben Stephenson, BBC Head of Drama

So return to your list and look at what is left. What is the story idea you feel most passionate about? Pick that idea and crystallize it into a logline.

The logline

A logline is a one- (or occasionally two-) sentence summary of a story which incorporates:

▶ the *who*
▶ the premise
▶ the plot.

This sentence will act as a mission statement for your script. Within that sentence you will need to establish who it is about, what they do and the problem they face.

Below is a list of hit TV shows and a single succinct sentence that distils the essence of those shows. You read the sentence and you know the show. Viewers (and commissioners) take an interest in a new show if it has an interesting premise. All of these shows ran for several seasons, but the logline could still apply to any episode of every season.

Breaking Bad Walter White, a timid chemistry teacher who discovers righteous self-empowerment through a life of crime.

Cold Case A female detective engaged in unravelling long, unsolved murder cases.

Doc Martin About a cantankerous surgeon who moves to a small Cornish village where he is to be the new GP.

Grey's Anatomy The lives, loves and lapses in judgement of five surgical interns at Seattle Grace Hospital.

Hustle About a team of con artists targeting various unsavoury
   individuals.

Joan of Arcadia Teenager visited by God in various guises.

Life Begins About a mother whose life is totally changed by the
   breakdown of her marriage and her need to find a job to make
   ends meet.

New Tricks: Comedy-drama about an unorthodox team of ageing
   detectives shunning modern investigative techniques in favour of
   old-fashioned graft.

The O.C. Arrival of underprivileged but streetwise teenager and
   the impact he has on the family who takes him in and on the
   community of Newport Beach, Orange County at large.

Scott & Bailey An exploration of the personal and professional lives
   of female detectives whose task is to track down killers.

Ugly Betty About an unattractive but talented young woman who's
   hired by a *Vogue*-esque magazine to stop the boss's habit of
   sleeping with attractive assistants.

Without a Trace About a New York-based FBI division devoted
   solely to finding missing persons.

Notice that all the descriptions are about a *who* – in most cases,
the main character(s). The second key element is the world your
character inhabits. The third element is a flaw or problem that the
who has to overcome. These are the three elements that you must
include in your logline.

> **Try this**
> **Now look at your favourite shows and try summing up the essence
> of that show in one sentence.** Do this as a party game where you use
> those single sentences and see if your friends can guess the shows. The
> ones that are easily and correctly guessed have the best loglines.

You will probably need several attempts to write the logline for your
own show but keep it as succinct as possible. Make sure every word
is needed. It will be the first reference that will entice someone into
reading your script. It will be included in your covering letter or
spoken aloud in a meeting or pitching session at a festival or during
a phone call. Competitions, too, often request a logline alongside the
script. As the name suggests, the logline will be used to log your script
on a company's system alongside the title.

The title

Titles are not necessarily the easiest to thing to create. Shows can often be developed without a title while others will have just a working title. The best TV show titles are creative and simple. The words used will need to convey something to the reader and entice the viewer.

New Tricks plays on the old adage that you can't teach an old dog a new trick. What is the show about? A group of old cops who are set in their ways and who solve crimes the old-fashioned way. *Hustle* with one word sums up the world of the conman. *Battlestar Galactica* tells us it is a big nebulous futuristic space show. *Blue Bloods* plays on a term used to refer to royalty and in this case it is the 'royal' family of the NYPD – the Reagans.

Other titles can refer to the central character(s) – *Chuck*, *Dexter*, *Luther* and *Scott & Bailey* – and because those characters are strong and interesting creations the name is enough.

Don't overcomplicate titles or use words which force the reader or viewer to refer to a dictionary to understand what you mean.

Try this

Below are synopses from two shows that have been seen on both sides of the Atlantic. For each synopsis I want you to write a title and logline. Try several for each. Later in the book we will reveal the actual logline and title of each show.

Synopsis 1

Alicia Florrick is a wife and mother who boldly assumes full responsibility for her family and re-enters the workforce after her husband Peter's very public sex and political corruption scandal lands him in jail. Pushing aside the betrayal and crushing public humiliation, Alicia starts over by pursuing her original career as a defence attorney. As a junior associate at a prestigious Chicago law firm, she joins her long-time friend, former law school classmate and firm partner Will Gardner, who is interested in rekindling their former relationship. The firm's top litigator and other partner, Diane Lockhart, likes Alicia's work and her connections, so she and Will award her a full-time associate position following a trial period. Alicia's rival for the post was Cary Agos, a clever young attorney, who, now bitter and vengeful, instead takes a job in the state attorney's office. Alicia finds an ally and a friend in Kalinda, the firm's tough and mysterious in-house investigator. Gaining confidence every day, Alicia transforms herself from embarrassed politician's wife to resilient career woman, especially for the sake of providing a stable home for her children, 14-year-old Zach and 13-year-old Grace. Now that Peter is back home and planning to run for office again with help from Eli Gold, his cunning image consultant, Alicia continues to redefine herself and her role in her family's life.

Synopsis 2

Emma Swan's life has been anything but a fairy tale. A 28-year-old bail bondsperson, she's been taking care of herself since she was abandoned as a baby. But when Henry – the son she gave up 10 years ago – finds her, everything changes. Henry is desperate for his mom's help and thinks that Emma is actually the long-lost daughter of Snow White and Prince Charming. Yes, the actual Snow White and Prince Charming. Even stranger, Henry believes that Storybrooke, the sleepy New England town he calls home, is really part of a curse cast by the Evil Queen, who has trapped fairy-tale characters in the modern world with no memory of their former selves.

Of course, 'seen it all' Emma doesn't believe a word, but when she gets to Storybrooke, she can't help sensing that everything's not quite what it seems. As Henry shows Emma around with the help of his fairy-tale book, the town and its inhabitants (like Henry's therapist, Archie Hopper, and the enigmatic Mr Gold) seem just strange enough to set off her already suspicious nature. She becomes even more concerned for Henry when she meets his adopted mother, Regina, who he suspects is none other than the Evil Queen herself!

Storybrooke is a place where magic has been forgotten – but is still powerfully close – and happily ever after always seems just out of reach. In order to understand where the fairy-tale world's former habitants have come from, and what ultimately led to the Evil Queen's wrath, you'll need a glimpse into their previous lives. But it might just turn everything you've ever believed about these characters upside down.

Meanwhile, the epic battle for the future of all worlds, modern and fairy tale alike, is about to begin. For good to win, Emma will have to accept her destiny and fight like hell.

Industry interview 2: the script editor

Hayley McKenzie is one of the industry's most respected script editors, having worked on shows such as Blue Murder, Casualty *and* Hollyoaks. *She also runs a highly successful script consultancy,* Script Angel, *where she offers a range of services to help writers with their scripts.*

Nicholas Gibbs: *What did your role as a script reader involve?*

Hayley McKenzie: When you're a script reader you're very much more looking at the quality of the writing. It's not your job to be considering a development slate or the needs of commissioners. Your priority is to serve forwards promising writing. And it is a fantastic job because of the sheer number of scripts that you read. I was reading for a lot of ITV companies, independents and for the BBC, doing drama and comedy. It was a really broad spectrum of genres and of quality of work because a lot of it was unsolicited, which meant that the writers didn't yet have an agent and often had very little experience.

NG: *So you became aware of what makes a good script?*

HM: Before I became a script reader I was working for Jane Tranter in BBC Drama Serials as a development co-ordinator so I was able to read all the scripts we had in development. So I had a benchmark. You've got a very clear idea of what a good script reads like and you see how that translates because you see that finished project on screen. Very quickly you understand what makes a good script and you can then measure other things against that. I think if you just read unsolicited scripts I'm not sure you'd get a great idea of what makes a good script – that's why writers need to read great scripts. You don't have to be working in BBC Drama to do that. There are lots of websites out there where you can download scripts of television dramas and films.

NG: *There are some scripts online that are earlier draft versions and some that are transcripts, which are not the same thing. My view is that transcripts don't serve the same purpose and aren't as useful as an earlier draft.*

HM: I agree. A transcript is much more a reflection of the director's interpretation of the script rather than what the writer delivered. They go through another metamorphosis once you go into pre-production and you get a director on board. The script performs a slightly different function at that point as well as it becomes a working document for a crew.

NG: *What is the most common mistake you see in scripts that can be avoided?*

HM: The most common is not having a clear idea of what the story is. I often go back to the writer, having read the script, and say 'What's the story?' Often they can't tell you in a sentence or two, and if they can't tell you then they probably haven't figured it out yet. It is so easily fixable and it's a kind of slight frustration because I feel that clarity of vision is what should be driving and creating the script. I think it's something that should have evolved before you send it out for people to have a look at.

NG: *Is that lack of clarity down to people sending their work out too early or is it writers suffering from the wood-for-trees syndrome?*

HM: I think that clarity of story is something that editors are really focused on and I completely get that often the writer in an early draft doesn't know what the story is; they're finding their way into this world, these characters. I am not a writer and I'm in awe of writers because they can sit there with a blank page and create something out of nothing in a way that I can't. I know many writers who find treatments [story summaries] really, really hard because they don't know their characters and story until they start writing the script and they start writing the dialogue. So I completely understand that a first draft is very much the writer's way of finding their way into that story. But as a reader what you would expect is that they will have gone through that process, read that first draft and started to work out what that story is and done a rewrite before they send that script out and say: 'This is my work.'

NG: *Writers on their own can't make things and the first person of contact is your friendly script reader who will make a decision on it. What does quality of the writing mean in that context?*

HM: Well, as a reader I was looking for one of two things. It might be that there is a great idea in here which has been executed poorly but the fact that they have come up with an original idea feels interesting even though it is a bit of a mess. Alternatively, it may not be the most original idea but if it is executed really well then I'm interested because this is someone who's really thought about what they're doing, really quite practised at the craft already; it might be that they have other ideas that are more original. Of course a script that does both is an amazing find, but if it is either highly original or brilliantly executed then I would recommend it.

NG: *How do you draw the distinction between, on the one hand, the good idea that has been poorly executed and where the writer may thrive on the feedback and, on the other, the writer with a good idea but who is ultimately not a good writer?*

HM: I think in the early stages you give quite broad feedback to see whether the writer can take those suggestions on board and rework the points on the script themselves. If you find they are struggling, then you give increasingly detailed notes in order to try and help them.

NG: *As a script reader, once you've made a decision, presumably that gets taken out of your hands?*

HM: Ultimately, that is the biggest frustration of being a reader and it is the thing that made me become an editor. There were projects that I was really excited about that I then passed upwards and then had nothing to do with because you then move on to the next batch of 25 unsolicited scripts to plough through in the hope of finding another gem. We have to let them go and that's quite frustrating. As you read more, you get a stronger and stronger sense of what you would do to help the writer to make that project even better, but you have to pass it on.

NG: *What kind of ratio would you get in a batch of 25 scripts that you would pass on? Is it the odd one or two, or even fewer than that?*

HM: Fewer than that. I think when you read more you become more confident in your judgements and you pass fewer upwards. I think in the early stages a nervous reader would pass lots of stuff up because they think there might be something there somewhere and you don't want to be the one who has missed it. But as you become more confident in your own judgement, you pass less on and that makes you a very valuable reader. The whole point of you is to stop the Head of Development having to read 25 scripts of the 25 that came in. You are only really picking the gems out.

NG: *When you become a script editor your role is as the writer's friend, if you like?*

HM: Your role changes enormously because it is no longer your job to judge the writer in the same way. Often someone else will have decided that this is the right writer for this episode of this drama and as an editor it is your job to help that writer deliver that episode. That's the be-all and end-all. No matter how difficult that might be for you or the writer. That's your job.

NG: *What about something like* Blue Murder*? Were you in from the outset of that or did you come in later?*

HM: If you're lucky, then you're in from the beginning of the process which means that it is your job to approach writers or agents. On *Blue Murder* we didn't do a completely open call. I approached particular writers and particular agents, but word does get round in the community that *Blue Murder* is going again and you're looking for writers. In addition to the people you've approached, you then get probably double the numbers who approach you with ideas. You're looking for stories that feel different enough from what you did in the previous series but still sit within the parameters of what a *Blue Murder* story has to be.

NG: *The rules of a particular drama are set up anyway. What is the process for you on a show like* Blue Murder*?*

HM: It's a hugely enjoyable process because it is very creative; it is very collaborative and you're starting from a one-line idea that's interested you. The process with the writer is a lot of conversations and developing the story.

NG: *At that stage are you sourcing known writers for a show like that?*

HM: At that stage it is about fifty-fifty. I would bring in writers I have worked with before but I am also open to ideas from writers I haven't worked with before but whose work I probably know. With *Blue Murder* it would be unusual to commission a writer with no credits because there is no hiding place with a show like that and the budget is substantial compared with an episode of *EastEnders* or *Hollyoaks*. So you need to be sure that the writer you commission will be able to deliver.

NG: *What is the schedule for an episode of a series like* Blue Murder?

HM: It is still pretty tight. When I first started on the show we'd just been greenlit and the first episode was due on camera six weeks later and we only had one script at that point and some first-draft treatments. So within a couple of months I had to have all five hour-long scripts pretty much ready to go almost from scratch.

NG: *Writers love deadlines because it is amazing what can be achieved. So generally speaking for an hour drama like that are you saying that is the norm that a script has to be ready to be shot within six weeks?*

HM: It could be six to twelve weeks depending on where they sat in the shooting schedule because obviously with *Blue Murder* you're single camera and shooting them as discrete hour-long films. We didn't shoot them in the order that they would TX [transmit]; we shot them in the order we knew we could get the scripts ready. It is about knowing your writers. It is about knowing the state of your stories, how much work you still have to do and knowing which writers can deliver at what kind of pace. We knew there was one story that needed a lot of work from a writer who was brilliant but not great at speed, so we scheduled that to shoot last. You've got to make those decisions pretty fast because you're already in pre-production.

NG: *If a writer is slow but brilliant, do you tolerate and accommodate that?*

HM: Whether you're on *Blue Murder* or *Hollyoaks,* your shoot date doesn't move and there comes a point where you have to shoot what material you can or you have to recommission. You have to get another writer in to deliver a script good enough in the time given because that time given can't be extended. You can't move a shoot because the script isn't ready, which is tough but quite motivating.

NG: *Do you get writers who think they have made it when they get on shows like* Hollyoaks?

HM: I'd say quite the opposite. I'd say every writer that I know is incredibly insecure and usually assume that this commission will be their last. There are very few complacent writers around that I know. Mostly, no matter how good they are and no matter how many times you tell them that they are good, they are never quite convinced and expect to be sacked any minute! Sometimes the problem is not complacency and that they feel they have made it but a belief that they are better than the show they are working on. I have come across that. Those writers tend not to stay on that show for very long.

NG: *One of the arguments against continuing drama is that the originality can be taken out of writers. In your experience is that the case?*

HM: No. I don't think it is the case, particularly over a reasonably short space of time. I think – and individual writers will have their own view on this – when writers have written on one particular show for a considerable number of years I think it is healthier that they have other things going on creatively at the same time. I think there is a danger of losing a sense of creativity and originality but only after a long period of time because the range of stories you can tell on any continuing drama is pretty broad.

NG: *Tell me about your Script Angel work? Presumably you get work of variable quality so what you're asked to do in response varies?*

HM: Yes, I have a very broad spectrum of clients. I do get a lot of inquiries and commissions from writers who are very, very new to it who are just finding their way into the industry. It can be the first time they have ever sent a script to anybody. Equally, I could be working on feature films and TV dramas with experienced writers. I think experienced writers also find a value in having editorial help to develop projects, particularly if they are moving into something new, like TV writers who want to move into feature films or vice versa. I am engaged by writers and I'm also being engaged by directors who have been brought onto projects and by producers and production companies as a freelance script editor through Script Angel.

NG: *When writers come to you they are looking to get their scripts enhanced and improved by having the script problems identified so they can be addressed?*

HM: New writers are often looking for a professional critique of their writing and their ability as a writer. Obviously, the advantage of being a script editor who is doing this as opposed to a script reader is that I don't just critique it but am able to offer suggestions on how they can improve it in a way a script editor would. I don't look at it as if I'm filtering their work as a script reader would. I look at it as if it's my job to help them develop this project to a point where it's filmable. That's how I come at any project whoever the writer is. I think there are some script consultants whose only experience is as readers. The feedback the writers are getting is often more of a reader's report. As a reader you're not giving notes to a writer to encourage them; instead your job is to produce a report that says well this bit's all right but this, this and this are the reasons you are rejecting it and the reader's report often forms the basis of the rejection letter. That is very different from a script editor's job which is to be much more constructive and more nurturing.

NG: *Do you get people who think: 'I'll do what Hayley says and then that's it, the script will be commissioned'?*

HM: I don't think so because as diplomatically as I can I'm quite honest about how much work needs doing. Again, I think that comes from years of experience in writing notes for writers. Your writer needs to be able to read those notes and understand how much work needs to be done but not feel like giving up. That's your job when you're delivering written notes because those words you put on the page they can keep reading over and over again and your job is to give them encouragement but not to be falsely hopeful about how good a script is. I think that another key is not always to offer solutions but instead to ask a lot of questions. What I never want to do is just criticize a piece of work and leave the writer kind of floundering as to what to do, but equally I don't want to be prescriptive and say if you just make this character do this here it'll be fixed. I offer possibilities to consider and ask whether that is the story they want to tell. What I'm doing now is less focused on written notes and more focused on discussions with the writer about the work.

NG: *You're trying to help the writer improve the script to the point it is seen in a favourable light?*

HM: Trying to improve it each time to the point where other people who are not being paid to work on it will read it and be interested in the project and the writer.

NG: *Of course there are limited places an unsolicited script can go?*

HM: If you engage somebody like myself at Script Angel, although that costs you money you not only get feedback to help make your script better but if we come across writers who are brilliant we will absolutely mention them to people that we know. I don't separate out Script Angel from the other aspects of my script editing work. If I take a job script editing on a show, I would happily recommend someone I'd come across through Script Angel if I thought they were right for it. Good writing, good ideas and good projects lodge in your head for ever. There are still times now when I'm having conversations with producers and directors and they say they are looking for a certain thing and I'll remember a project I read ten years ago by a writer I haven't been in touch with for five years – you don't forget it and you don't stop thinking about those writers.

NG: *What are the things you find in scripts you don't like seeing?*

HM: I'd like to get to the end of the story and I should be able to sum up what that story was. 'It is about a girl who...' It might have lots of things going on underneath that or running alongside that but it should have one driving story that you can sum up at the end. It might be subtle and only a small shift but I'm looking for a clear sense of story. I also don't want to have to ask what the point of that scene is. How has it changed anything? What have we learned about those characters? Has the story moved on? If it hasn't done any of those things, then why is it there?

NG: *The writer should be asking those questions to a degree?*

HM: The thing is to think of it as a process and as a writer you do have to learn to become brutal about your own work because a scene that was fantastic three drafts ago becomes redundant because of the bigger changes you make in the story or the way you're telling the story or the focus of the piece. If it doesn't sit well anymore, it has got to go. No matter how much you love it. It's the hardest note to give as well. To be an editor on the phone and say: 'I love this scene; you know I love this scene but you know it has got to go.' A good writer might be keeping that scene in because they love it but when you have that conversation they recognize the truth of the note. The bottom drawers of good writers are littered with brilliant characters, ideas and scenes that just didn't work in the script anymore as the project developed.

www.scriptangel.co.uk

5

....

Creating characters

In this chapter you will learn:
- *how to create an engaging, fully rounded protagonist*
- *how to create drama by making different aspects of a protagonist's life come into conflict*
- *how character shapes the development of a scenario.*

The most important element of all television drama is the characters. If your characters don't come alive, don't leap off the page, then no matter how good your premise the script (and drama) is destined to fail. The importance of character cannot be understated. By researching audience reaction to new shows, organizations such as the Television Audience Programme Evaluation have learned that the decision viewers make to commit to a series is based mainly on character appeal rather than story content.

Good, engaging, memorable characters are a must for any script. Good characters can overcome a poor premise but poor characters can kill a great premise. For example, compare smash US musical series *Glee* with UK musical flop *Britannia High*. The success of *Glee* can be attributed to the characters (and the music). It is certainly not the storylines which are predictable and are there to hang the songs on for each episode. It is the characters that really make the show, from the Streisand-wannabe Rachel to the sassy Santana to the naive comic brilliance that is Britney.

Think about *Britannia High* and, if you did watch it, can you recall the characters? Go on. Name me one of the characters? Go on. Nope, it's not going to happen because the characters weren't strong enough (among other things) to resonate.

Make a list of the most memorable TV characters from television drama. Separate them into UK and US characters. To help you, here is a list of five from both sides of the Atlantic:

UK	US
DCI Gene Hunt (*Life on Mars*)	Jack Bauer (*24*)
Harry Pearce (*Spooks*)	Dexter Morgan (*Dexter*)
John Luther (*Luther*)	Gaius Baltar (*Battlestar Galactica*)
Sherlock Holmes (*Sherlock*)	Alicia Florrick (*The Good Wife*)
DC Rachel Bailey (*Scott & Bailey*)	Detective Jimmy McNulty (*The Wire*)

What makes those characters interesting? They are all, to varying degrees, larger-than-life but more importantly quite complex individuals who are deeply flawed in some way. So, your characters need to be complex, compelling, strong and distinctive. They have to *matter* to the audience. Let's now look at how to create such characters and let's start with your hero – the protagonist.

The protagonist

The protagonist is your main character – your hero or heroine. It is the character the viewers are going to tune in for every episode. In Chapter 4 we talked about the logline for your idea and saw that invariably any story is about a 'someone who…'. So, who is your *who*?

Writers approach creating their characters in many different ways but with the same goal – namely, by the time they write the script they will have a set of characters they know so well that they will act consistently as themselves and not merely to service the plot.

You are telling a story about a particular part of a character's life. So you, as the writer, will want to know how they came to be by the time that we first meet them on screen. Create a biography, a backstory if you will, for that character and list everything of importance before the story begins, including their upbringing, their career, their relationships and their education. Look at their favourite things in terms of possessions, hobbies and so on. You can make an extensive list – most of it will probably never be used in a script but which will nonetheless help in creating a three-dimensional character.

Character background sheet

1 Full name (and aka)
2 Age (date of birth)
3 Single/married/partnered/divorced/widowed (and to/from whom)
4 Children (age) – and the character's relationship status with them
5 Best friend
6 Education
7 Occupation and responsibilities
8 Are they good at their job? What are their strengths/weaknesses? Do they like their job?
9 What is their dominant attitude – that is, how do they see and interpret the world?
10 What do they do in their free time? With whom do they socialize?
11 What are the significant moments of their life?
12 How have those moments affected them?

The questions above are opening gambits of inquiry. The answers you provide should provoke other questions that need answering as you delve deeper to create your fully rounded characters. It will help to colour their attitudes and behaviour so that they act consistently within your script.

Now look at the character as we meet him/her at the start of the script. Everyone has three distinct parts of their life that tend to be kept separate but which may occasionally overlap or collide: the public, personal and private personae. When that happens, conflict is created.

PUBLIC PERSONA

This is where we see our characters most – namely, in the public arena. They are usually defined by their occupation or position.

What is their job? In cops and docs shows it is very obvious that the character's job in these circumstances will have a profound effect on the drama but it applies equally to any occupation.

Think of the protagonist's start to their working day – their daily routine from the point the alarm clock starts the day through to how they get to work. Do they travel by public transport? If so, is it by bus or train or boat or plane? Or do they travel by car? Is it their car or a company car? Is the car new or second-hand? Do they get a lift in a friend's or work colleague's car? Is it because they share fuel costs? Is it because your protagonist doesn't own a car or because they have never learned to drive or have been banned from driving? Do they walk to work? Do they even have a job to go to?

Just looking at that commuting aspect of their day can reveal so much about their status and wealth (or lack thereof) and potential problems in their lives. Immediately, you can get some insight into that character and this leads to further questions and yet deeper insight. If they have been banned from driving, for instance, is it because they are reckless? Is it because they drink? Is it because they couldn't afford to insure the car? Is money tight? Are there debts?

What about the job to which they are commuting? What does their actual job involve? What position in the work place hierarchy do they hold? How do they get on with their work colleagues? How do they get on with their boss? Are they responsible for any staff? Do they deal with anybody from outside their company or organization? Do they deal with the public? What is their attitude to the public? How long is their working day? How do they commute home? Do they bring work home? Are they on call? Do they like their job? Is it a vocation or just a job?

In all aspects of their lives, ask questions of your characters and answer them. Those answers will help contribute to a full-rounded character by the time you start typing.

PERSONAL PERSONA

What is your character's personal life? Are they married? Do they have children? Are they divorced? What age are the children? What is the character's relationship with the husband/wife and kids or ex-partner? What are their relationships like with other family members?

Look at the character's social circle. Who are their friends? How do they interact? Where do they meet and what do they do? What are the character's perceptions of their friends? Who is their best friend? Do they fancy their best friend's wife? How long have they known their friends? Are they part of a group of childhood friends who have grown up together? Are they a newcomer to an existing group because they have moved to a new town for a new job? What music do they like? What football team do they support? To what degree do they support that team – just via the scores, via the TV or as a season ticket holder?

With family, friends and work relationships, examine how those relationships unfold and change as you tell your story.

PRIVATE PERSONA

The other aspect and arguably the most important of a character's existence are the moments when they are alone. This is when we can see what they are really like and see what they really feel. Are they crying alone in the dark? Are they secretly drinking? Do they obsess over their secret folder of cuttings about their brother's death? Does their brave public persona crumble when they lay awake at night? Do they have a sinister secret? Do they have a vice that is socially questionable? The classic case of the wildly different private persona in contemporary TV drama, of course, is Dexter Morgan, in the successful Showtime series *Dexter*. Let's look at this protagonist a bit more closely:

Dexter Morgan

In public Dexter Morgan is an excellent forensic scientist for the Miami Police Department. He is a well-respected professional who has a reputation for specializing in blood work (there is an irony). The perceptions of Dexter as a social, personal animal are mixed. He is not an innately social animal but he has a perceived close bond with his foster sister, Debra, and is in a relationship, of sorts, with Rita and her children. This makes him appear normal and disguises his true self, which we only see in private or when the audience hears his true thoughts through the use of voiceover. This private or true Dexter reveals that he is, in fact, a serial killer and responsible for many, many murders.

Now Dexter is the hero of the story. Come again? I know. A serial killer is the hero. How can that be? People watch the show in their millions and root for the serial killer. Why is that? Dexter has a private dilemma, a dramatic tension that sees him fight between his own base urge to kill because it satisfies him and the morality he has inherited from his late adoptive father. Dexter's solution is to fulfil his murderous desires by killing people who can possibly deserve it. Who deserves it? Other killers, especially murderers who appear to have escaped justice or who threaten to unveil Dexter's dark secret.

In that light, Dexter is almost a superhero. In a perverse way he is doing something good by doing something bad. He has a terrible secret, a character flaw that he can never share or he will face the punishment that society inflicts on those who kill.

Finding a flaw in your lead character will make your protagonist human. Serial killers are publicly portrayed as being the personification of evil. In Dexter's case he is a human being, like everyone else, trying to find his place in the world, to find acceptance – a universal theme.

> *'What if I created a surgeon who wasn't cut from the usual cloth? He would have to retain the God complex. I want a surgeon to have a God complex. You don't take the top of somebody's head off and start fiddling inside their brain without a fairly inflated view of your own worth. And I wouldn't want it any other way. But I was interested in somebody unexpected being a surgeon. Somebody without the accent and manner you might expect, somebody who might look and sound more like the man who came to repair your washing machine. A man who was a deity at work and all too mortal at home. That, surely, would make a good starting point for a drama. A surgeon who was both God and Everyman.'*
>
> Peter Bowker, Creator and Writer (*Monroe*)

Think of your major characters and their flaws and vulnerabilities. Make them interesting. It is from those character blemishes that you will maximize the drama, the story. This element should feature in your logline. The protagonist needs a goal – a task to fulfil – which is set up in the opening pages by the Inciting Incident (see Chapter 8).

Once you have answered the questions about your protagonist, the answers may help you to get an angle on him or her. You could go into further detail and that will be down to your personal way of working. Remember all this character biographical work need not be included in the script but it will shape the way you write your character in terms of dialogue, action and decision making. Remember your protagonist will have to be proactive.

Introducing characters

When you introduce your character for the first time in the script you will need to distil all this knowledge into three or four words and/ or phrases that encapsulate that character for the reader. Below are some examples of how characters have been introduced in scripts:

Captain Jack Harkness (*Doctor Who*) He's impossibly handsome, dashing – the jawline of Dan Dare, the smile of a bastard.

Rose Tyler (*Doctor Who*) She's 19, her bedroom's a mess, she's got another bloody day at work, and she's so much better than this.

Willow (*Buffy the Vampire Slayer*) She is shy, bookish and very possibly dressed by her mother.

Xander (*Buffy the Vampire Slayer*) He is bright and funny and will one day be suave and handsome. Till that day arrives, he'll do the best he can with bright and funny.

Mickey Stone (*Hustle*) Late thirties, sexy, inscrutable.

Ash Morgan (*Hustle*) A rather scruffy man in his early fifties, but looking much older, careworn.

Sam Tyler (*Life on Mars*, UK) Smart, lithe, mid-thirties. If he were a flavour, he'd be spearmint.

DCI Gene Hunt (*Life on Mars*, UK) Emerges like a bear from a cave. Leather jacket and Texan cord tie. He shoves an Embassy No 6 into his mouth.

Olivia Dunham (*Fringe*) She's 32 years old, beautiful but real. A deceiving innocence.

Peter Bishop (*Fringe*) 35, handsome, fit. A quiet glance and you see a swagger. Drive, confidence. A close look shows a sadness.

Don Draper (*Mad Men*) Early thirties, handsome, conservative, and despite his third old fashioned, he is apparently sober.

These brief introductions distil the character when we first meet them. These descriptions offer a kind of pithy character statement that gives you the essence of the character which should guide you through the script. They may, of course, become changed by the experiences of the story. Those of you who watched *Buffy the Vampire Slayer* witnessed Willow undergo a dramatic change from when we first meet her, from shy mummy's girl to powerful lesbian witch!

This is a process you can apply to all your characters but you will need their reason for being – namely, what is it that your character *wants* within an episode or within the series and what do they actually *need*? We'll look at this idea more closely below.

Wants

Wants are what your characters' goals are for your story. In detective stories the police want to solve the crime, catch the perpetrator and see justice be done. In medical dramas the doctors and nurses want to cure the patient, make them better and send them home. In relationship dramas a character may want to escape a marriage while another character may want to save a marriage.

Identify from the story you're telling what is it that each character wants? Do they all want the same thing? Does everyone agree? Let's hope not, or else there will be no conflict and without conflict there is no drama. Ask what obstacles are in your hero's way to try and stop him getting what he wants. (We will look at this again in Chapter 8.)

You want your stories to be populated with characters with differing views, social abilities and outlooks. Each character needs to serve a different purpose. Your characters will need to react differently to the same stimulus.

If you've ever seen somebody walk into a plate-glass shop door, you'll recall how the different shoppers reacted to this incident. The first thing you'll note is the sound of laughter from people who loved the slapstick nature of it. In contrast, there will be the person who will go and help the unfortunate individual. No laughter from them; instead they empathize with that person because they may have hurt themselves and will go to help. There will also be other people who go to react in a similar way but are not the first to reach the victim. They will hover, ready to help if needed, along with other people who hover because they want to look as if they are helping.

There will be people who would have heard the crash of the person's head as it hit the door and will be curious to know what happened. They will ask any eyewitness and will either react with laughter, dismissiveness or sympathy depending on their personality.

Then there will be the individual who knows, out of the corner of their eye, that something has happened but do not want to get involved. They keep walking, head down, pretending nothing has happened. In character terms that individual is the most interesting because it begs the question: what has happened in their lives that they block out an incident like this?

And what of the victim? Would it change the attitude of any of those people if it wasn't just a stupid accident? What if the victim had been pushed? What if the victim had become ill or had a condition that affects their balance? Would people's attitude change either in the moment or after the incident when this information becomes known?

Characters need to have different approaches and attitudes. Look at *Life on Mars*. The character of Sam Tyler tries to use the modern policing techniques of the twenty-first century to solve the crime of the week. DCI Gene Hunt's approach is very different and very un-pc for modern tastes. They both have the same goal but deploy different attitudes and strategies to achieve results. The resulting conflict creates engaging drama.

If you go back to the first synopsis at the end of Chapter 4 you may recognize the show. It is *The Good Wife* which stars the excellent Julianna Margulies as our heroine Alicia Florrick. In the synopsis several regular characters are referred to and their role in relation to Alicia, namely, as ally or enemy. For example, the young lawyer Cary Agos is an enemy since he loses out to Alicia for the full-time associate position at the Chicago law firm. His vengeful and bitter motivation will be different to Alicia's.

Needs

Your characters' needs do not usually coincide with their wants. In terms of television storytelling, needs are often unachieved until the very last episode. The workaholic detective/salesman/doctor/builder may need to concentrate on his family for a happier life rather than work every hour that God sends. Sexual tension between two characters can sizzle over several series, but consummation is constantly postponed because other things get in the way. (If they do get together, be pretty sure they won't be together for long because an ex-lover or wife will turn up, or one of the characters will be abducted or die!)

You may also have guessed that our second synopsis in Chapter 4 was from ABC's *Once Upon a Time*. The show's heroine is Emma Swan who wants to be with her young son, Henry, whom she gave up for adoption. However, what she needs is to accept and believe what Henry tells her – that she is the daughter of Snow White and Prince Charming and that she has a destiny to save all the fairy-tale characters that are trapped and live in Storybrooke.

Try this

1 Create a scene in which an attempted mugging takes place.
2 Select one of your characters and place them in the scene.
3 Write the scene.
4 Now rewrite the scene but this time using a different character.
5 Repeat, replacing your character with another of your characters.
6 You will end up with several versions of the same scenario but with different results. This will be as a result of each character's individual reaction to what happens to them.

Key advice

▶ Characters are at the heart of successful TV drama.
▶ Make sure you know your character back to front, even if everything you come up with doesn't make it into the script.
▶ Make sure your character is multidimensional – not all good or all bad, but a real human being with needs, wants and inner conflicts.
▶ When you first introduce a character, make sure they make a splash!

6

Dialogue

In this chapter you will learn:

- *that dialogue must be used as sparely as possible and must always move the story forward*
- *how speech rarely states the literal truth about the speaker but hides a plethora of hidden motivations*
- *how to create individual voices for each of your characters*
- *how dialogue is shaped not just by personality but by context, too.*

Dialogue is well-edited conversation. In television drama, a visual medium, dialogue accounts for around half of the script. Within any script the dialogue has to move the story along, convey key information and help define character. If you can achieve more than one of those things at the same time, then you are honing your craft to a higher level – and that impresses.

When you write any word of dialogue you need to ask yourself whether it is really necessary. If you can show the same thing with an image or through action, then go with the image and/or the action rather than the spoken word.

Script dialogue may appear natural but the reality is that it is an artificial construct which, hopefully, is not noticed as such. Superfluous words should be cut and the characters should only say what they need to say, though in their own way. Good dialogue is precise and economic and not obvious. Think of it as if you, the writer, who has to pay for every spoken word you use. You will then use only what is necessary and effective.

In 1974 the Moody Blues, one of the biggest and most successful bands of the time, stopped working together. The reason the band members cite is that, after an extensive world tour in which they lived in each other's pockets all day and every day, they stopped talking to each other because they knew what the other guy was going to say. The band members resorted to code – 'Conversation number 15' or 'Joke number 9'. In that bizarre situation they did not expend any unnecessary words because they already knew them. That is what you have to do as a scriptwriter.

With any piece of dialogue you need to ask *why* your characters are saying those words. Very often what is said is not what is really meant and can be contrary to what the character is thinking.

All dialogue is lies

Characters in television drama should never be seen to say what they mean. All characters have secrets, be they scandalous or inconvenient, that they don't want to be revealed. Everyone wants to present themselves in the best light. What a character's secret is and how they choose to conceal that secret adds layers to the character and reveals the truth about their feelings.

Most dialogue scenes in television drama are duologues – where two characters have some form of conversation. However, there will always be one character that drives the scene. Perhaps they want to convey information to the other character or get information out of the other person. In either case, it should not be an easy task.

Dialogue should not be on the nose. That is, it should not be obvious. It should be about what is not said (subtext) – about the difference between *what* is said and *why* it is said. The truth is people always want to be seen in the best light and often dance around the real topic in the room. Arguments between husband and wife over the husband not taking out the garbage again will not be the real cause of conflict between the couple. It could be the affair the husband had two years before for which the wife has never really forgiven him or the debt they have or the behaviour of their wayward child or their dead relationship. Two cops working side by side have an unspoken love for one another which reveals itself through their day-to-day banter. In television drama it is actions that show the truth, not the spoken word.

When people greet each other at work in the morning and ask 'How are you?', the reply will be the stock 'All right', 'OK', 'Well, you know'. Of course, you don't know but you can sense that *something* is wrong.

In David Shore's hit medical series *House*, Dr Gregory House, played by Hugh Laurie, has the mantra 'Everybody lies'. It is a good mantra to adopt when writing dialogue. In emotional terms, people rarely say what they mean because, if they do speak the truth, there will be an impact and consequences. Watch any drama and there will invariably be a big secret which has to be kept concealed. This creates dramatic tension. Drama is driven by the revelation of that secret and, once that secret has been uncovered, then nothing will be the same again. Characters will put in a conscious effort to sidestep, misdirect or lie outright to avoid talking about or revealing the secret. Sometimes the secret is an open one but confronting it is avoided because there will always be the raw emotion that burns at the heart of a character's being.

Speech patterns

One of the common problems new writers have when writing dialogue is that they tend to write every character using the same speech patterns, namely their own. The result is that every character speaks in the same voice, which also happens to be that of the writer.

Writing clear and distinctive dialogue is one of the hardest but one of the most necessary skills to master in writing for television. You will have to develop an ear for dialogue and the only way to do that is to *listen* to people. Listen to conversations in public places and take note of the rhythms and cadences of real people talking. You will have to master the art of getting those unique voices down on paper.

There is an oft-quoted test that everyone in the industry from script readers to executive producers use when reading scripts – and writers should use it, too. The test is to cover all the character names in your script and just read the dialogue. For any piece of dialogue, from the distinctive way it has been written, you should be able to work out who is saying those words.

So how did you get each character to sound different without giving each character a different accent? (Never, ever do that!) This goes back to how you develop your characters. Think about their status, their job, their education and, most importantly, their prevailing attitude.

In the pilot episode of David E. Kelley's *Harry's Law* the second act opens with an exchange between the show's heroine, Harriet 'Harry'

INT. JUDGE WINSTON'S COURTROOM - MORNING

Not yet in session; lots of LAWYERS, CLIENTS, PEOPLE milling about. We find HARRY, with D.A. JOSH PEYTON, forties, leaning over the prosecutor's table, rushing through some last second paperwork. He speaks quickly.

> PEYTON
> (not looking at her)
> What do you mean, let him go, you
> kidding me, you kidding me?

> HARRY
> I'm not saying let him go without
> consequences--

> PEYTON
> Yeah, just without jail, lemme tell
> you, counsel, jail is the only
> consequence these people understand.

> HARRY
> These people?

> PEYTON
> Oh, please, gonna make it a black
> thing now, gonna make it a black
> thing, gimme a break, gimme a break,
> third offense, I'll give you a year,
> best I can do, best I can do.

> HARRY
> Yeah, the thing is if he gets any time
> he'll get expelled from college...

> PEYTON
> Wish I could help you.

> HARRY
> It doesn't really sound like you wish
> you could help me, Mr. Peyton. In
> fact, it sounds more like you wish I'd
> bugger off. Is that what you really
> wish?

> PEYTON
> What, you wanna make sport of me now,
> that it? That it? 'Cause I gotta
> tell you, you're a slightly bigger
> target at the moment, you think I
> don't know the book on you?
> (MORE)

(CONTINUED)

Figure 6.1 Scene from the pilot episode of Harry's Law © *Bonanza Productions Inc.*

```
CONTINUED:
                        PEYTON (cont'd)
            Hot-shot corporate lawyer suddenly
            goes cartoon-happy, now you're here
            defending drug addicts?  What's that?
            What's that?
                  (to a PASSING COLLEAGUE)
            How you doin', Sal,
                  (back to Harry)
            What's that?


                        HARRY
            Mr. Peyton.  This boy needs a break.


                        PEYTON
            Yeah, well, don't we all, lemme tell
            you, if you think you're gonna get no
            time for a three-time loser -- not
            gonna happen, not gonna happen.


                        HARRY
                  (almost avuncular)
            Look.  I'm no expert on criminal law.
            But more times than not, trials come
            down to which lawyer a jury likes more
            and my feeling is they'll look at me
            and they'll look at you. And they'll
            tumble to something you know all too
            well and which I'm beginning to
            suspect.


                        PEYTON
            Which is?


                        HARRY
            You're an asshole.

A beat, as he stares.  And breaks into a thin, sickly smile.
Like a cat who's about to swallow a canary.
```

Figure 6.1 (cont.) Scene from the pilot episode of Harry's Law © Bonanza Productions Inc.

Korn, and district attorney Josh Peyton. Read this now (Figure 6.1). Notice how the dialogue for both characters is distinctively different and how that reflects their attitude and traits as characters. As mentioned above, most scenes are duologues where one person wants something. Here Harry wants something from Josh but Josh doesn't want to play.

Harry wants a deal that will save her client from jail. Josh wants to expedite the case because to him, on the evidence, it is a clear-cut conviction. Josh's speech pattern, the repetition of words and phrases reflects an inflexible but exasperated man who is under pressure but knows he has the power. Harry, in contrast, tries to make Josh see beyond the letter of the law and make a morally right decision. Harry's language is deferential and polite up until the point she realizes she's not getting anywhere; at that point she defaults to her smart alec riposte.

The outlook of the character can have an effect on the words and phrases that they use. Think about the following:

▶ Is your character someone who loves talking about themselves and whatever the subject will turn the conversation to them?
▶ Does your character always talk and answer in questions?
▶ Is your character a man or woman of few words?
▶ Is your character shy?
▶ Does your character have an inflated view of themselves?
▶ Does your character have a wide vocabulary and love to show off their love of words?
▶ Does your character flirt with everyone they meet?
▶ Is that flirting harmless banter or uncomfortably sexual or simply crass?
▶ Does your character want to impress others?
▶ Does your character have poor social skills?

Verbal ticks and context

People have verbal ticks. They may overuse certain words or use the wrong words. In our excerpt from *Harry's Law* above Josh repeats certain phrases to emphasize his exasperation with Harry and her request. He does that each time he is being dismissive or making a stand.

Other characters may use certain favourite phrases for all sorts of reasons. Here are some examples to consider for your characters:

▶ People may have phrases they repeat to seek validation – 'Do you know what I mean?' 'To be perfectly honest with you…'
▶ They may be someone who never uses names and refers to everyone as 'mate', 'lad', 'son' and so on.
▶ They may curse or swear a lot.
▶ They may have an idiom that is characteristic of their age group. How many times do teenagers use the word 'like' for example?

- They may speak in sporting metaphors.
- They may rely on banter and funny lines.
- They may talk in a matter-of-fact fashion.
- They may talk in a transparently manipulative way.
- They may speak in a condescending way.
- They may be cynical.
- They may have a 'glass half full' attitude.
- They may have a permanently sunny disposition.
- They may complain about everything.

The context in which your characters speak also has a bearing on the character of their speech. The speech may be more formal in a work context. For example, when a police detective gives a press interview to talk about a particular case his or her language is very neutral and matter-of-fact (they are trained to do that). However, they will speak about the same case with their colleagues in a very different manner. Similarly, a teacher will teach a room full of pupils without resorting to expletives, but swear like crazy in the staffroom. Once again, here we have the difference between the professional and the personal.

When thinking about context, consider the following:

- Where is the character?
- Who else is present?
- What are the circumstances of the conversation?
- Is the character on the offensive or defensive?
- What is their state of mind?

Good dialogue should do more than one thing. It should be more than the literal words spoken. When any character speaks there is always a reason for doing so. As a writer you should ask why does any character speak? What does the speaker want? Once you know that motivation, the words the character says aloud will colour their choice of words and their delivery.

Try and avoid clichés in speech. Where you see one, try and find a way of reworking the speech or rephrasing them. Dialogue on television is a construct so the audience expects it to be clever, erudite and insightful.

Try this
Exercise 1

▶ Choose a fairy tale such as The Three Little Pigs or Little Red Riding Hood.
▶ Choose your protagonist to retell that story in their own words to group of friends as if it was a real event.
▶ Choose another of your characters to tell the same story in the same context.
▶ Do likewise with all your other major characters.

At the end you should have several different versions of the same story as told by each of your characters. The words used and the way the story is told will be different. You may have a comic character who tells the tale as a joke or another who dwells on the gruesome aspects or another who uses it as a warning to others.

The voice of the show

The other aspect that affects the type of dialogue is the particular language of the show itself. From *Buffy the Vampire Slayer* to *The Wire* in the US, from *Coronation Street* to *Top Boy* in the UK, each show has its own language and language is context.

Industry interview 3: the scriptwriter (I)

Lisa Holdsworth has written for a host of top British shows including Emmerdale, Fat Friends, New Tricks, Waterloo Road, Robin Hood *and* Midsomer Murders. *Like so many writers she is also developing her own authored series. Here we discuss life as a working writer.*

Nicholas Gibbs: *How did you get your first break as a scriptwriter?*

Lisa Holdsworth: I didn't study. I never did a writing course. I did a degree in Film Studies down in London. Once I'd done that I came back to Leeds and worked for four years in factual television making science and history programmes but all the while I was writing stories. I'd written stories from being really tiny – I was a terrible liar as a child!

NG: *A great way to make stories then?*

LH: Yes, absolutely making stuff up! While I was working in factual, I met the son-in-law of Kay Mellor [UK scriptwriter well known for her work on soaps such as *Coronation Street* and *Brookside*]. I took my opportunity: 'Would your mother-in-law read my script? And could you slip it into the bottom of the pile.' He must have put it on the top of the pile, bless him, because she read it. Later on, actually at the head-wetting party for his new son, Kay took me off to one corner and told me everything that was wrong with the script. I'm thinking: 'Well, obviously I've got no talent.' Then right at the end of this speech she said: 'Actually, I think it is a really good script. You've got something. Let's talk about you may be doing something for me.'

NG: *How did Kay help you?*

LH: At the time she was making a show called *Playing the Field*. She got me a scriptwriting trial on that. I was completely untried and all I had was this one script to show anyone. Tiger Aspect, the production company, said no but also said I did a really great script trial. About six months later I really didn't want to work for the company I was working for anymore. I rang Kay up and she took me on as her personal assistant, which was a dogsbody job. I'd pack her bags and answer her phone and feed the cat and all that kind of thing. I worked out of her house. At the time she had just finished making *Fat Friends* which had been a massive success and she said she didn't want to make another series and she had said everything she needed to say. David Liddiment, the controller at ITV at the time, rang up and suddenly we were making Series 2 and it was all systems go. That weekend I went home and wrote a treatment for an episode. I didn't even know it was a treatment. I wrote what I thought was a story for an episode. At that time we knew Meera Syal wasn't going to come back into the show and there was a gap for a new family. On the Monday I shoved it under Kay's nose and said: 'I've done this – is this any good?' By the Friday Tiger Aspect said yes and I was commissioned on the understanding that, if I couldn't handle it, they would take it off me and they'd give it to another writer. That never happened.

NG: *So you had this one* Fat Friends *script. Did you expect new assignments to roll in?*

LH: It was almost a year from that commission. I'd got myself an agent, Georgina Ruffhead at David Higham Associates, but she was selling an absolute unknown who had apparently written this *Fat Friends*. It could be rubbish. Everyone was waiting to see what it was like. I wanted something that was regular work because I was aware of how inexperienced I was. I said I really want to get on a soap and she said, 'You'll be lucky – they are closed shops at the moment.' I ended up temping with the National Health Service for a while. When the episode went out, because it was Lisa Riley – it was her first straight acting role since leaving *Emmerdale* – it got lots of publicity and it was choice of the day in lots of newspapers. It got shortlisted for the new writing BAFTA that year and suddenly people were asking to see me and one of them was *Emmerdale*, which suited me. I knew the characters and, bless him, Steve Frost (or Steve November as he is now) called me in for a meeting. He put me in the story office for a month before I started, to get me up to speed and to see how the series worked. It was a fantastic experience. I loved it, working to four in the morning bashing out stories. It was really a good experience and it did me a favour. I went on to the team and wrote three probationary scripts. I just hit the ground running. It was my area. It was the Yorkshire accent which I know, with stories that I knew, with characters that I knew. It was really a good move to get on that show.

NG: *So how long were you at* Emmerdale?

LH: I was at *Emmerdale* for three years. It was the best fun and the best credit up until the moment it wasn't. I think there's a moment when you put your fingers on the keyboard and you write 'Interior. Woolpack' and you absolutely don't want to do it. You're not giving your all. Don't get me wrong. *Emmerdale* can be a pain in the arse but I absolutely loved it and I was lucky I was doing the show when it was riding on a bit of a high. I loved the politics of the story office; I loved the dynamics of it and then it gets to a point when it is not a challenge anymore and it's a bit dull.

NG: *Where did you go from there?*

LH: By that time I'd had the first approach from *New Tricks*. I'd pitched and had a pitch accepted. I did a treatment and had the treatment accepted. Suddenly it was a brand-new world for me and again it could have gone horribly wrong but I decided it was time to leave *Emmerdale* because I'd had enough. I never want to be stale. I never want to write just for the money, which is a beautiful concept but the reality is everyone has to do it for the money because they have to pay the mortgage.

NG: *You started* New Tricks. *Did you step into that easily?*

LH: Actually, I was terrified. I never wanted to be a police writer but we had a really good police advisor on the show. I was coming in on Series 3 and it's a very male-dominated show and, as much as I'd like to say it makes no difference what gender you are, I think it does. I was walking into a show where it was all boys apart from the lovely script editor, Nicola Larder. It worked because of the comedy aspect of it and the warmth of it, which I think a lot of other police procedurals don't have. I could do the banter of the four main characters. Tom Sherry, who was my producer, said I never got the story right in the first drafts but I got the warmth. He must have known I'd get there eventually. I'd be banging my head on the desk, going 'I don't know who did this murder and I don't know how I'm going to prove it', but I'd get there eventually because the dialogue would be strong, the characters would be strong.

NG: *What sort of timescale did you have for an episode?*

LH: When I first came in – it's less now – it was six weeks for first draft, but by then you would have thrashed out a treatment, and treatments go backwards and forwards to the point where you think: 'I can get a script out of this.' You get four weeks for the second draft and then as many drafts as it takes up until the first day of shooting. I've done an episode that took me six weeks to write in total because another writer's episode fell apart mid-series. They rang me up and said: 'Have you got anything to go for the next series?' 'Yeah, I've something kicking around.' 'Do you think if we put you in a hotel for a week you could write four drafts in a week?' 'I'll have a damn good try.' I'm not claiming it was the best writing experience in the world but it got done. It varies but there's much more luxury on *New Tricks*. I'd say from scripts to the notes it's about six months, from first going in pitching to first day of shooting.

NG: *How is your treatment writing? Has it become more refined?*

LH: It became more pragmatic and more aware, particularly on *New Tricks*. I know what can or can't be done. When you do go in to talk about a new show, particularly an existing show, it's best to ask what story they don't ever want to be pitched again because there is always one. Ask yourself: 'What are my constraints, basically?' I think constraints are good for writers. I think to be a fan of the show you need to be critical of it. You watch it and see what's wrong with it. I don't want to see that in my episode.

NG: *How do you handle exposition?*

LH: On *New Tricks* there are two ways: one is the white board of death where they are standing at the white board, and they are putting the pictures on, and you plough through it as quick as you possibly can. You write long and then you edit down and edit down and edit down, so you get to a point when the audience is going to get what we need from it. The other approach is the banter approach – chat-chat-chat. They're talking about Chinese takeaways but we're stripping in facts about other stuff. The most nebulous skill of writing is dialogue. You either get it or you don't. That sounds an awful thing to say but the rule you live by is: 'All dialogue is lies.' People are sarcastic, people use hyperbole, and people use metaphors and similes and all those kind of things. Again, I've never learned it; it's just something I've always done. My family talks like that all the time. So there's a big part of first drafts you read back and think: 'No human being would reveal this information in this way. How can I bury it? How can I twist it?' I think the one part of writing you can't teach is dialogue. Don't get me wrong: I think there are some professional writers out there who get regular commissions who couldn't write dialogue if their lives depended on it, because there is some absolutely terrible dialogue out there which is often covered up by intricate and brilliant stories. I don't come from the intricate; I come from the character and it's just something I've always done.

NG: *After* New Tricks *what position did you feel you were in then?*

LH: You've proven yourself at that point because the reality of soap writing is no one takes you seriously. The BBC don't care I've written 40 hours of *Emmerdale*. With *New Tricks*, because you generate the story and investigations using existing characters, it is a bit of a showcase for you. You're saying 'Look what I can do!' *New Tricks* did start to get me noticed. I moved from *New Tricks* and then did *Waterloo Road* then *Robin Hood*. The next game is to get my own show. It has been seven years of development and near misses, but that's where I am now – which is going in and pitching ideas and having the balls to do it. Knowing that I love *New Tricks* but I don't want to do it for ever. *Robin Hood* wasn't going to go on for ever; *Waterloo Road* most certainly wasn't going to go on for ever. So it's generating ideas and watching the markets and seeing what's out there. That's where the real pragmatism comes in and it is where you can sometimes feel that you're selling your soul because you go to meetings and you go: 'What do you want?' 'What we want is a relationship drama.' 'Oh just so happens I've got one.' The ideas I've got that are in my drawer I love them but I won't put them in front of a producer to share because there's no market for them. I don't want it to be butchered and turned into something else.

NG: *All the commissioners say: 'Don't try to anticipate what we want, just pitch to us'?*

LH: Absolute crap and I don't mind you quoting me. At best, it is naive saying, 'Please just pitch what you think is great.' That's fair except we all have kids to feed and mortgages to pay. I could pitch some crazy idea set in outer space – it might get a commission as my absolute dream project but I don't want it to get crushed. Once it is out there, it's out there. If it's not the right time for it – timing is everything – then I'm not going to pitch it even though it's my absolute dream project. I look round the commissioners and think: 'You won't get it.' There's no money for it or someone else has just made something similar and it was awful and you've just salted the ground for me.

NG: *Do you like American television?*

LH: Oh God, yes. They do develop characters and have a bigger canvas that goes over a series. I think a hidden gem of an American series is *The Good Wife*, which is delicious. It was a traditional, slightly political, legal drama and then builds and builds and builds. It's stunning. With a 22-episode series you can really develop that. When you compare that with *Silk*, which was very good, but the characters sometimes had to revert to cliché because you've only got a small canvas. You have to go to the whole 'she wears red lipstick and she has sunglasses and, oh look, isn't she brave coming back to work after having a miscarriage' thing. It could have been a much better slow-burn story with high stakes and we would see so much more of the character.

NG: *Is that to the detriment of British writers?*

LH: It's almost patronizing of British writers to constantly remind the audience about character traits – oh yes, she loves red lipstick and smokes a fag! Once you've established trust, the audience will go with it. I call it the UK Gold effect, which is where – I don't think I'm giving any secrets away on *New Tricks* – we make sure each episode is stand-alone so they can be repeated on UK Gold or on Alibi or on Dave or whatever. And my opinion of that is, if you're waiting around until it gets on Dave, then to hell with you! You should have watched it when it was on BBC1.

NG: *What is your writing day?*

LH: I get up at six and do a couple of hours. I say I do a couple of hours. Those first few hours of the day are, you know, messing about on Twitter and my Facebook page. All of that is what I call grooming behaviour for writing. All those things you've got to get out of the way, read your email – all that kind of thing. I'll go off and have some breakfast and come back to the desk about nine o'clock. Then the real writing starts, though you think you needn't have got up at that time because you've done nothing at all! I set off and I write until lunchtime. The last session, from about half past two until I pack it in, is not terribly productive. The reality is, if you condense down the actual time it takes to write, it's not that much really and I've never got to the end of a deadline and not thought: 'If you hadn't fannied about, you could have finished a week early. Why did you have to go on Amazon and look at those things? Why did you have to do this? Was that Twitter conversation about last night's *Doctor Who* really that important?' I would say, if you're really struggling, then turn the Internet off. I still have the radio going... Maybe because I worked in an office for four years but I can break off and come back, break off and come back.

NG: *When you write your first draft are you great planner or do you splurge it out?*

LH: I don't scene-plan. I don't do: scene one this is going to happen; scene two this is going to happen. I write in prose and just in paragraphs and then that's as far as I go. I'll write the story to the end. Sometimes in the middle of writing scripts I'll have to go back and retype where the big moments are etc. I'm just doing that at the moment. I'm writing a pilot for ITV. I sat down and tried to write the treatment but something was stopping me and I know the big moments are not dramatic enough yet. Those can be moments of desperation where those nagging voices at the back of your head are saying 'This isn't right!' Sometimes you have to go away and just refresh it. You know you've planned it but it is not working, so go back and have look at it and re-strategize. It's the hardest thing to do. It's the hardest thing in the world to start again and say it's not working. If you work with a really good script editor, they might give you the old praise sandwich, telling you what is brilliant but they'll also tell you something is not right. If you're really upset with notes and you won't change a word, you're not going to get a repeat booking.

NG: *Are you perceived as a particular type of writer?*

LH: I think all writers get typed. The thing I get is: your voice is warm and funny and you have the northern thing going on. There is a certain amount of pigeonholing which can do you good. If you put in a relationship drama and they think she does warm and funny, that's great. It is about knowing the prevailing attitude about your writing. Sometimes it is about saying 'You know the stuff that I do? Here is some more of it.' That's marketing yourself. I do write warm and funny very well. The ideas that I am producing tend to have a warm and funny spin on them but it's because I love character. I'm never going to be friends with Quentin Tarantino. I wouldn't pitch the British *The Wire* – that is someone else's job. The problem is I'm normally seen as a safe pair of hands, not an innovator. What you get on the swings, you lose on the roundabouts. There is something to be said for sticking something under someone's nose they didn't expect to get. I've got a dream project that is a Saturday teatime show which is very different and if I pitch it, it'll be 'Oh I didn't expect that from you!' You can trade on your history but it can be a bit of a constraint sometimes.

NG: *What advice would you give writers?*

LH: It is the advice Kay Mellor gave me. Don't kick an idea around, or write a treatment or script with an imaginary commissioner, producer, script editor or even the audience sitting on your shoulder saying 'I don't buy that'. Just write and write and write and then go back. And you'll inevitably think, 'I can't believe I've written this! It's a load of garbage,' but you can change it without anyone ever knowing. That first draft is literally an exercise in *finishing* something. You're not a writer until you've finished something. Nobody has to see that first draft. They see draft 1.4.

7

Creating a world

In this chapter you will learn:
- *how a successful drama depends on the creation of a convincing and consistent world for your characters to inhabit*
- *the importance of thorough research, preferably (if possible) by direct experience of the real-life equivalent of your world (e.g. a hospital if you are writing a medical drama).*

With any original script you are creating a world, a world in which to play out your stories. That world could be a hospital (*Casualty*, *House*), a stately home (*Downton Abbey*), the streets of London (*Whitechapel*), alternate universes (*Fringe*), a specific city such as Baltimore (*The Wire*) or a cobbled street in northern England (*Coronation Street*).

The world could occupy a particular time period: *Call the Midwife* (1950s), *Downton Abbey* (early twentieth century), *The Tudors* (the reign of Henry VIII) or the futuristic *Battlestar Galactica*. In some shows like the fantasy drama *The Game of Thrones* the era is indeterminate or vague but can be likened to the European Middle Ages. *Grimm* is set in the present day but with a dark fairy-tale twist.

Research is very important. So, if you are intending to set your story in the past, make sure you do your homework and know how things looked and worked, namely, the rules of the period. Likewise, if your drama is a police procedural or legal, know how the police work and/or the court system works. If it's conmen, know how the world of the conman works.

The world your drama is to inhabit needs to be established and can be very specific. Think of the number of different medical shows set in and around a hospital. In the UK there is BBC's *Casualty*, which is set in an emergency department, and its sister show, *Holby City*, which is set in the same hospital but centres on the surgical wards. ITV's *Monroe* centres on the neurosurgery department, where the eponymous hero works as a brain surgeon. BBC1 daytime drama *Doctors* is set in a GP surgery while Channel 4 comedy-drama *Sirens* is about an ambulance crew.

There are many shades of medical drama as there is for any other kind of drama, so you need to establish the exact nature of your world quickly.

One of the biggest hits on British television has been *Hustle* on BBC1. Created and written by Tony Jordan, it ran for eight series between 2005 and 2012. The series' opening sequence in the first episode (Figure 7.1) not only introduces the main characters but quickly establishes the world we are in – that is, the world of the conman. It is also a prime example of that the scriptwriter's maxim 'Show, don't tell'.

Hustle was such a success that it inspired the showrunner John Rogers to co-create the US hit *Leverage*, which was about a group of con artists and thieves who exact revenge on the powerful and corrupt.

With every world there are rules that define the parameters of the world for the audience and you as a writer. It is the rules you set that will bring a consistency to your storytelling. For example, if you set your drama in a modern-day hospital, your characters have to operate in a realistic hospital environment (watch how many times the medical staff wash their hands on *Holby City*, for example) and display the appropriate medical knowledge. No one should be finding the cure for cancer. A futuristic hospital may be dispensing the cure but that's a different drama with different rules.

With the pilot script you are establishing the rules that are intended to act as a blueprint for a serial or a potential returning series. Audiences (and readers) dislike inconsistency and rule breaking for the convenience of the plot. It is about knowing your world because your characters should certainly know it because they are supposed to have lived in it every day of their lives.

Research the world in which you are going to set your story. If it is a medical drama, go and see how a hospital works, and talk to the

EXT. CITY STREET - DAY 1. 1258

Sunshine. City's worker ants streaming towards us - making
their way to offices and shops;

A moment. City life. Then;

Pick out one figure, someone less ordinary; someone who doesn't
fit.

MICKEY STONE, late thirties, sexy, walks along - surrounded by
worker ants, inscrutable.

He sees huge bill board advertising lipstick - giant pair of
red pursued lips with the slogan *"Never give a sucker an even
break"*.

He looks to camera, wry smile.

INT. POSH RESTAURANT - DAY 1. 1310

PETER WILLIAMS, a businessman in his mid-forties, his suit and
jewellery oozing money, sits at table with business colleague.
Colleague signs credit card slip for bill.

Colleague stands and puts £25 cash tip on tray. They shake
hands and colleague leaves. Once his colleague is out of
sight, WILLIAMS checks he's not being watched then sneakily
reaches over and takes £20 note from tip.

This is seen by avuncular looking ALBERT STROLLER at nearby
table.

INT. POSH RESTAURANT - DAY 1. 1314

WILLIAMS leaves restaurant and walks through bar.

ALBERT watches him go. Leans back to maitre de desk and spins
reservation book round to check name.

EXT. CITY STREET - DAY 1. 1320

Smart polished shoes - pan up expecting to see city gent,
instead it's ASH MORGAN a rather scruffy man in his early
fifties, but looking much older, careworn... Walking along row
of shops with heavy shopping bag...

No-one pays him any attention, a face in the crowd.

He looks at camera.

Figure 7.1 Opening sequence of Hustle, *Series 1, Episode 1 © Kudos Film and Television*

INT. POSH RESTAURANT. BAR - DAY 1. 1322

WILLIAMS sits at bar, something falls to his feet, he leans
down and picks up a classy cigarette lighter.

As he straightens up, he finds himself looking at ALBERT
sitting on next stool. ALBERT smiles as he takes lighter back,
offers to buy WILLIAMS a drink.

As ALBERT turns to order drinks, he looks into camera through
mirror behind bar and touches his nose.

INT. POKER ROOM - DAY 1. 1323

Been a long night, five poker players in various states of
sweaty, smoke stained disarray, battle weary. Pan around table
to DANNY BLUE, babyface, small stack of chips left, he looks at
player opposite; waits for him to make his play.

DANNY looks at camera, then throws remaining chips into pot,
shit or bust.

EXT. CITY STREET - DAY 1. 1325

Ash Morgan turns the corner, proceeds on his way.

INT. OYSTER BAR - DAY 1. 1326

CU of glossy magazine ad, idyllic, somewhere in the sun, palm
trees, white sand, the Caribbean...

Pan up to reveal STACIE MONROE, mid to late twenties, a real
head turner, legs look though they finish just below her
armpits... Sits sipping coffee watched by group of four young
city guys standing nearby. Others egging one of them on;

STACIE aware of this, but continues reading... Then;

STACIE closes magazine, puts money on bar and gets up to leave,
the city guys watch as she swivels off stool.

Legs.....Egged on by his pals, the smarmiest of the city guys
stands, God's gift...blocking her way - she bumps into him.

INT. CITY GUY'S CLOTHING - DAY 1. 1327

Slightly in front of camera is beautifully manicured hand, long
red nails.

SLOW MO as it glides under jacket, across freshly pressed
shirt, and into blackness of inside jacket pocket.

Figure 7.1 (cont.) Opening sequence of Hustle, Series 1, Episode 1 © Kudos Film and Television

```
FADE TO BLACK.

FADE IN: AS;

Slender fore and middle fingers pull wallet out of blackness
and into sunshine.

INT. OYSTER BAR - DAY 1. 1327

STACIE smiles at smarmy city guy who looks delighted at the
collision, before she carries on her way to door.  He grins
inanely at his mates.....As STACIE reaches door, she puts
wallet inside magazine.

Look to camera, leave.
```

Figure 7.1 (cont.) Opening sequence of Hustle, *Series 1, Episode 1 © Kudos Film and Television*

staff, the patients and so on. If your drama is a police procedural, look at how things are run and talk to policemen, detectives, lawyers. Whatever the nature of the drama, be it medical, political, sporting, and so on, research the world – not by watching TV but by going to talk to people in the real world.

Writer Ronan Bennett just did that for his excellent Channel 4 series *Top Boy* about the drug culture on a Hackney estate. Writer Sally Wainwright spoke with Diane Taylor, ex-police detective and co-creator of *Scott & Bailey*, about what life was really like in a serious incidents unit and about being a woman in the police. In *The Wire*, creator David Simon and his writing room investigated all aspects of Baltimore public life to create what became an outstanding series.

Even the makers of sci-fi space shows such as *Star Trek* and *Babylon 5* all looked at what was possible. Know your world and know it well.

Key advice

▶ Create a credible and consistent world for your characters to inhabit – even if it's a sci-fi drama.

▶ Set out the rules (and limitations) of your world as quickly as possible and don't break them!

▶ Research the subject area of your drama as much and as directly as possible – a day spent in a courtroom is better than a week spent in a library reading about courtroom procedures!

8

Structure

In this chapter you will learn:
- *about the four-act structure used widely for the 'commercial hour' drama episode*
- *how the first ten pages – essentially Act 1 – is crucial for hooking your audience (and the script reader)*
- *about teasers, tags and cliffhangers.*

You have created compelling characters, a fascinating world and an intriguing premise, and now we examine how you are going to put it all together as a script.

The structure of a story is simple: it has to have a beginning, middle and an end. For television drama the structure is broken down into acts, whose beginnings and ends, on commercial television, are dictated by the advertising breaks. However, the act-based structure is equally applicable to the uninterrupted drama of a public service broadcaster like the BBC or a subscription-based broadcaster such as HBO.

ITV, C4, Sky and many US network shows work to a four-act structure while the BBC, influenced in no small way by John Yorke's Writers' Academy, utilizes five acts.

In this chapter we will look at the elements of a 'commercial hour' drama because it is probably the most used, both in the UK and US. The structure is dictated by advertisement breaks which provide natural markers in the construction of your script. However, the insights into structure you will gain here are equally applicable to shows that have no commercial breaks because producers, particularly in the US, will be looking for them to be syndicated on channels that do have ad breaks.

First, let us break down the TV commercial hour – see Table 8.1. In the US there can be four or five ad breaks to the hour while in the UK there are three ad breaks. The timings shown in the table are approximate and are there as a guide. Any act can be longer or shorter than this but the overall running time has to be met. Remember: one page of script approximately equates to one minute of screen time, though that will depend on your writing style and the style of the show you are writing.

Table 8.1 The four-act structure used for the 'commercial hour' drama

	Act	Appox. length	Script length
UK	Act 1/teaser	12 mins	10–15 pages
	ad break		
	Act 2	10/11 mins	10–15 pages
	ad break		
	Act 3	12 mins	10–15 pages
	ad break		
	Act 4/tag	10/11 mins	10–15 pages
US	Teaser	1–4 mins	1–3 pages
	ad break		
	Act 1	10–12 mins	10–15 pages
	ad break		
	Act 2	9 mins	10–11 pages
	ad break		
	Act 3	10–12 mins	10–15 pages
	ad break		
	Act 4	8 mins	9–10 pages
	ad break		
	Tag	1–2 mins	1–2 pages

This is merely a guide and, because it is drama, it is not set in stone. You may write acts that are shorter or longer than 15 pages. Just write what is necessary for your script. The only rule is that you have to hit the running times of the broadcast slots. Try and write as close as you can to the time length of the slot, though you should err on writing longer because it is easier to edit down than pad out.

The BBC, particularly through its continuing drama shows, is an advocate of the five-act structure and suggests a rough guide of 12–14 pages per act. However, there is no reason why acts can't be longer or shorter – for example, if a six-page third act suits you, then write a six-page third act, though obviously the time will have be made up elsewhere.

Let's now look at each part of the structure in more detail.

Act 1

The first act of any drama is about the set-up and tends to be the longest act. It establishes what the story is about and the dramatic needs of the main characters. It also sets out the tone of the piece. Generally speaking, a first act will be 12–15 pages long. However, for the sample spec it could be argued that you should consider the **first ten pages** as your first act as that is what the script reader will initially judge you on.

In part because of the sheer volume of unsolicited scripts that land on the reader's desk, and in part because any story in any script has to grab its audience from the outset, the script reader will make a judgement based on the first ten pages. If the first ten pages don't grab the reader, they are certainly not going to want to read the other remaining 50 pages. Why would they? After all, you don't persist with a dull book or newspaper article if it you don't enjoy or have any interest in it.

The first ten pages are therefore enormously important, especially for the new writer. It may be brutal, it may be unfair, it may even be short-sighted, but it is the way it is. Bite the bullet and embrace the 'first ten page' rule and see it as the rocket fuel that could propel the reader to read the whole of your script.

So what do you need to do in those opening first ten pages?

Television executives have a mortal fear of the hovering forefinger above the remote control. One drop of that digit and your episode is dead in the water. No licence fee, no advertisers, no subscribers. There is a plethora of channels which the ever-demanding viewer can access and so every channel wants to grab them. And they have to grab them at the outset. This applies particularly to television drama – the most expensive type of programme to make.

You will need a strong opening image or engaging words to grab the audience. Indeed, you need to jump straight into your story and cut the 'once upon a time'. Don't introduce Little Red Riding Hood preparing food for Granny. Have Little Red Riding Hood attacked by the big bad wolf – this is exactly how *Grimm* introduced itself on to our screens.

The advice 'hit the ground running' is often given to new writers. This needn't be taken literally of course, although Paul Abbott did exactly that in his excellent thriller *State of Play*. The spoken word can be equally effective if the words are engaging. Toby Whithouse's *Being Human* opens with the words of Annie:

ANNIE

Everyone dies.

(beat)

Actually, can I start that again?

(beat)

Everyone deserves a death.

These intriguing words lead into an opening sequence then proceeds to show the three main characters, Mitchell, George and Annie, engaging with 'death'. Mitchell is 'sired' by the vampire Herrick in World War I and in turn sires a woman in the present day. George is discovered in the aftermath of a brutal attack on a man in his secret state as a werewolf. Annie is shown staring lifelessly after she has seemingly fallen down the stairs, blood spreading out from her head.

In Abi Morgan's excellent *The Hours* set in a 1950s television newsroom we open on the moment Freddie is making a plea to change the face of televised news in Britain. These are all moments that grab the viewer from the outset, pulling them into the world of the drama without any preamble or explanation. The opening sequence, the first few minutes of your drama, will show *how the world is* in an engaging manner. This is the **teaser** – the opening sequence that often occurs before or as the opening credits roll. American television is a big user of the teaser, which can be anything up for five pages long, though it forms part of Act 1.

> *'In TV the first act is the teaser. It is literally the teaser – it is the big question. And you're drawn into it. Of course then there's another question and it goes on and on.'*
>
> J.J. Abrams (*Lost, Alcatraz*)

Within those opening ten pages and the sooner the better, there also needs to be what is termed an Inciting Incident.

INCITING INCIDENT

The inciting incident is the reason why the viewer is watching the drama – it is the spark of the premise. In detective shows it is the discovery of the body (or actual murder). In both series of the Patrick Harbinson-created *Kidnap and Ransom* the Inciting Incident is when a prisoner exchange goes wrong. In Ron Moore's *Battlestar Galactica* it is the attack by the Cylons. This moment, usually seen in the first five pages, fuels your story for the episode (or episodes or series).

OTHER JOBS ACT 1 HAS TO DO

Apart from providing the teaser and the Inciting Incident, there is plenty of other work for Act 1 to do...

Who is it about?
Remember your logline – that one sentence that crystallized your idea – it included the *who*. In the first ten pages you need to establish who the hero is and our way in. Is your story about a ghost, werewolf and vampire (*Being Human*) or a hostage negotiator (*Kidnap and Ransom*) or a woman released from prison after a 15-year sentence (*Unforgiven*) or a pair of identical twins (*Ringer*) or as group of lottery winners (*Syndicate* or *Winners and Losers*).

We need to see who they are and...

What they are up against

The Inciting Incident indicates the problem your hero or heroes face: the need to solve a crime; the need blend into society and hide; the need to deal with becoming rich; the need to save the human race. From that you can infer who they are up against, namely, the enemy. The enemy could be an invading force, a kidnapper, a murderer, the public, the police, family, friends or even themselves.

The world

You have created the world of your drama but now you have to establish it in the first ten pages. Not only the world of the character as a police detective, hostage negotiator or doctor but also the geographical world they inhabit. It could be a space station, a particular city or particular building.

The when

You need to establish the *when* of your world. Is it in the past, present day or the future? Is it historically true or generic? For example, *Game of Thrones* is arguably a medieval tale but is not set in a documented historical time and place.

The rules

The rules of the world need to be established quite quickly, particularly if there is a twist to that world. In *Grimm* the twist is that the present-day world is occupied by fairy-tale characters in disguise. In *Being Human* the twist is that ghosts, vampires and werewolves live and prey among us. *Fringe* is based on the concept of alternate universes and that differences apply depending which universe the episode is set in.

What type of show is it?

You will need to make clear what kind of show it is. What genre is it? What is the show's tone? If it is a thriller, the first ten pages should be thrilling; if it is a comedy-drama, be funny; if a horror, be scary; if it is an action story, let's see some action.

All this is a lot to do in ten pages, but it is what you have to do to propel the reader on to the eleventh page and beyond. It has to be a page-turner.

At the end of Act 1 you will need to create a plot-based **cliffhanger** or emotional revelation that will entice an audience back after the ad break and that will keep the script reader turning those pages.

Act 2

Each act has to serve a purpose and you want to be clear about what you want to achieve. In basic terms, your destination within each act is the end-of-act cliffhanger. The end of Act 2 (in a four-act episode) will be your **halfway point** (aka **midpoint**), which marks the furthest point your hero gets from achieving his or her goal.

By the start of the Act 2 your characters and tone should be well established. During the second act it is all about the obstacles in the way of success. These obstacles should create conflict and build tension and propel the story along. Your characters are pushing forward and are having increasing amount of success until suddenly they hit the barrier of failure or an unexpected outcome. By the end of the act a major event or revelation occurs that is so significant it redirects the story in a different direction and creates new problems. It may be a point when a character is in jeopardy or takes a step backwards from their goal.

The problems of Act 2 may have been resolved but they also create new and unexpected obstacles.

Act breaks

The end of each act is very important in terms of storytelling on commercial television. You have to make sure you entice the audience back. In the UK an ad break can be up to three minutes and 50 seconds long and so that last image, that last revelation, that moment of jeopardy, needs to be big enough to linger in the mind long enough to make the audience return.

Act 3

Act 3 makes things even harder for your characters. They are battling against the odds and they now look like they're heading for failure. Be clear what purpose the act serves and the problems that have to be overcome. Basically, a good tenet of television writing is to create characters you love and then make their lives as hard as possible –

make them suffer! If a problem is solved, then a new one should arise or the resolution of the problem itself should produce unexpected results. The end of Act 3 is the all-or-nothing moment – when the character(s) and we the audience realize that there is only one outcome or confrontation left and we are propelled into the final act.

Act 4

Act 4 is all about the resolution. The plot builds to a climax and is resolved. By this stage of your episode everything needs to be heightened to fever pitch. Make sure, with regard to your A story in particular (see Chapter 9), that there is a climax, a big finish – or, if it is a serial, that you have what I call an 'Oh shit!' moment when something is revealed that changes everything.

The best illustration of this is the closing episode of Season 3 of *Battlestar Galactica* ('Crossroads, Part 2'), which climaxes with the revelation that four regular characters are not as they seem, coupled with the return of a character previously thought to be dead.

THE TAG

In old-school terms this is the epilogue. It occurs at the end of the script when everything is wrapped up. It may pay off a plot point or it may be a running gag. A tag can be as little as one to two pages long but forms part of the final act.

Key advice

- ▶ The four-act structure can be a very helpful discipline for the beginning scriptwriter.
- ▶ Remember, though: the four-act structure is a useful tool, not a commandment set in stone.
- ▶ The first ten pages of your script are crucial – remember: hit the ground running!
- ▶ End each of Acts 1–3 on a cliffhanger – you need to entice the audience back again after the ad break.
- ▶ The final act should be about providing a resolution.
- ▶ However, there may well also be a final 'twist in the tale' to help reel the audience in for the next episode or series.

9

....

The story

In this chapter you will learn:
- *that most TV dramas are structured around two, three or even more storylines*.

It is incredibly difficult, and rare, for a single hour of television drama to be sustained by a single story. The norm is for the episode to be sustained by at least two other stories that interact with and/or are linked thematically to the main plot. Each episode tends to be made up of an A, B and C story. Some of the more ambitious dramas –*The Wire*, for example – have even more stories on the boil and certainly some BBC dramas have D and E strands.

The A story will focus on your main characters, the hero or protagonist, and the story outlined in your logline for the script. The B story may deal with the personal lives and problems of the main characters which may relate either thematically or directly to the A story. The C story could be about the lives of the supporting characters.

As a rough guide, this is how those stories will break down in your script:

- ▶ A story   60%
- ▶ B story   30%
- ▶ C story   10%

These percentages are only a guide and the various story strands may take up a greater or lesser proportion of the script depending on the stories you want to tell.

Below is an illustration of how a three-strand story could work in terms of the four-act structure as a ratio:

	A	B	C
Teaser	1	1	0
Act 1	3	1	1
Act 2	3	2	0
Act 3	3	2	1
Act 4	2	1	0

Sometimes the teaser is all about the main A story. The C story may be told over a single scene in each act. The B story may be resolved by the end of Act 3. It all depends on how you choose to tell your stories.

Questions to ask of each storyline

▶ What is the story about?
▶ What is the theme that links the storylines?
▶ Does each storyline make sense? (If you separated each storyline as a stand-alone sequence of scenes, would it be self-contained?)
▶ What does each character do?
▶ What does each character think?
▶ What is the complication – the drama – of each story?
▶ How is tension created and how does it lead to the next action in the story?
▶ What is the core problem that has to be overcome?
▶ What choices does the main character make in each story?
▶ What consequences result from those choices?
▶ Do characters take responsibility for their actions?
▶ How does each storyline end?
▶ What is the timeframe for each story?

Try this

1 Watch an episode of your favourite TV show.

2 Note down how many stories there are and, using one sentence for each, what they are.

3 Write down all the key moments in each story and approximately when they happen.

4 Identify how many acts there are and what happens at the end of each act. (Note that in the UK the ad breaks for US shows do not necessarily signify the end of an act. The end of an act is usually indicated by a fade out / fade in.)

5 Do the same again with a different show.

6 From both examples, you should now have a guide to television story structure. Use them to help you plot out your stories.

Key advice

▶ Your main storyline – story A – will probably have to be supported by at least one other storyline – story B, C, etc.

▶ A rough ratio of time spent on the A, B, and C stories will be 6:3:1.

▶ A typical A story may deal with an event in the protagonist's professional life, while a B will relate to their personal life.

Industry interview 4: the scriptwriter (II)

Marc Pye has been writing for film and television for the past 14 years and has written more than 100 hours of serial drama. Among his television credits are The Street, Holby City, EastEnders, The Bill, Waterloo Road, The Royal, Holby Blue, Doctors, Moving On, Echo Beach, River City, High Road *and RTE's* Fair City. *He is the author of two novels,* Lollipop *and* Rewire *(Sceptre) and his three short films –* Baldy McBain, Last Legs *and* Instant Credit *have all premiered at the Edinburgh International Film Festival.* Instant Credit *was also selected for the Newport Beach Film Festival, LA in 2004. His first feature,* Act of Grace, *starring Leo Gregory, David Yip and Jennifer Lim was released in April 2012. His second,* Between Weathers, *went into production the following month.*

Nicholas Gibbs: *How did you break into television drama?*

Marc Pye: I used to hound everyone with my scripts. Any indie I found in the phone book; even if they did documentaries I still sent it to them. I used to work in Boots the Chemist in Glasgow's Sauchiehall Street and Scottish Television was just up the road from there, so most lunchtimes I'd head over there with my scripts and hand-deliver them. There was a script editor there who would read my stuff and would write back to me with encouraging letters. They all basically said the same, that the opportunities were limited and, although he liked my writing, I'd be better off trying to get on a long-running show, but he appreciated how difficult that was. A couple of years later he was made producer on *High Road* and I got a call from him to come in and have a crack at writing a script for the show. I wrote it, he liked it and I got on the show and went on to write 29 episodes.

NG: *Your first gig was writing for the* High Road *and you later wrote for* River City – *what was that experience like? And in practical terms what was the writing process?*

MP: High Road was pretty easy now I look back at it. They gave us scene breakdowns which were pretty prescriptive. I didn't stick rigidly with it and would always slant it so there was more of a hook to the scenes or I'd merge scenes if I didn't think they were moving on the drama.

They allowed me a lot of free rein as long as I stuck to the restrictions, like what set was available and so forth. It was all a great learning process. I then went on to *The Bill*, where I learned a lot more but the principles remained the same, like leaving a scene or a part break on an unanswered question or jeopardy. As it was a cop shop, that was ideal. With *High Road* I had been spoiled, as we usually only did two drafts. With *River City* we worked from a storyline, again with an A, B, C story, wrote a scene breakdown, went to script and did between three and five drafts. I did that for a few years and wrote 56 episodes.

NG: *You then joined* The Bill *which was, by then, a one-hour show. How did you find writing for the longer form? Unlike the* High Road, *presumably you had to pitch stories of the week and create original guest characters. What was the process for that?*

MP: Yes, there was a script editor who liked my work and she was working at an indie. She got me meetings with her boss and we got talking about possible ideas and I did some pitches and stuff, then she went to BBC Wales and called me up one day and asked me to come up with ideas for drama in Wales, which I did. It was called *Rewire* and was about two Liverpool electricians who go to work in Wales, but Jimmy McGovern's *The Lakes* was due to come out, which had a Liverpool guy working away from home, so as there was a similarity we couldn't do it, so I later wrote it as a book.

She then moved on to *The Bill* and I got a call, saying 'I'm at *The Bill* now. Do you watch the show?' I didn't, so she suggested I should and then start pitching ideas for it. I did that for six months and had a few near misses and then one day a story got through called 'Sweet Sixteen', about girl gangs. It was great to be able to create guest characters who could give the regulars a run for their money. I'd always liked the character Rod Skase, who was a bit sure of himself and thought of himself as a ladies' man. Girl-on-girl crime and girl gangs targeting guys was on the increase, so I put the two together. I had him undercover, cocky, thinking he could flush this girl gang out, but they are too clever for him and turn the tables on him, abduct him, belittle him and totally mess with his head. I really wanted to get the mileage out of the character and by the end of the episode I'm sure he wasn't the same character!

The longer form wasn't and has never been an issue for me. Some stories are best told in one hour, some in 30 minutes. I really don't have a favourite. With *The Bill* we were given a story document with an A, B and C story and wrote a scene breakdown from that, with part breaks in it. I think we did about five drafts once the breakdown had been OK'ed, but then it became a lot more when the way of working changed and it became more of a serial drama. When I started on the show they were stand-alone episodes, but then the personnel changed and it became a different show with more of a serial running through it to engage the viewer and increase the figures. There was a lot more work involved, as storylines would change at draft three, four, five and sometimes even be thrown out, and that meant the work you had done was redundant and you had to start from scratch. It happened to all the writers and it's something that still happens on shows if something isn't working. You've just got to knuckle down and get on with it.

NG: *Tell me how your episode of* The Street *came about? Would it be fair to say that was your first original TV script in that all the characters and premise was yours?*

MP: The show was originally called *The Likes of Us* as a kind of working title. I'd been working with a producer in Manchester who liked my work and he called me one day, saying he and another producer who I'd been sending my work to had been discussing me. The exec from Granada, who was doing *The Street*, was looking for 'a gritty northern writer', as they put it. She had called them to ask if they knew of anyone who would be suitable and they recommended me. Granada called me to tell me to expect the call. I didn't really expect anything to come of it, till a script editor called me up, told me about the show, and that it was going to be set in Liverpool in the exact area that I grew up in and that Jimmy McGovern also grew up in. The area was a bit rough, so to write a story set in the streets I grew up in really appealed to me. She said if they liked the idea and it all went ahead that I would be working with Jimmy as a kind of script editor and mentor and asked did I have a problem with that. I think you can guess the answer. The idea I pitched was a story of injustice, about a respected teacher who is out jogging, needs to take a leak and goes into the bushes. He's seen by a small girl and her father thinks he is a pervert. The teacher panics and runs off. He later gets identified at the school parents' night and it all goes horribly wrong for him. It was my first original TV script and got me a lot of work and attention as a writer after it went out. As it turned out, they moved the series to Manchester but it worked just as well.

NG: The Street *was an award-winning series and you said that you used 'The Flasher' as a sample to try and get a job for a film but the reader didn't think it was emotionally engaging. Could you recall that story? I think it is an illustration of how fickle the industry is and the fact that nobody knows anything!*

MP: I think the reader will know who they are so I don't want to mention the show, but when they were filming *The Street* I met Arthur Ellison, who wrote the final episode of Series 1. He came up to me and said, 'I got your script to read and I was halfway through and the tears were running down my face. I though how the hell is this poor guy going to get out of this?' He had to put it down and call Jimmy to say he loved the script but tell him the effect it was having on him. I think the fact that we are emotional creatures as writers had something to do with it and I know Arthur won't mind me telling that story, as it's a great example of how we can move people through our work. When the show went out I had text after text, call after call and tons of emails all saying the same thing – that they cried, were choked or so moved by what was happening to this family, for the injustice the character suffered. And then there were also the tears of joy when it's resolved for him. But this reader read it with a view to me writing for the show and said it failed to emotionally engage them, so thanks but no thanks. Hey-ho, best to quote William Goldman on that one!

NG: *What was your experience of* The Royal *and* Holby Blue? *Although both were new series they were spin-offs and were very different in tone. How do you 'tune in' to a show's tone?*

MP: Ken Horn, who was my producer on *The Street,* went on to do *The Royal,* which had been running for a while (*The Royal Today* was the new one) and called me up and asked would I like to write for the show. It had a great charm to it and reminded me of *High Road* and it was great to be working with Ken again so I said yes. The thing I found was it was quite gentle and not all action-packed so I had to calm down and remember my *High Road* days, but it went really well and I did two episodes, but then like *The Bill* it sadly went off the air. I'd always admired Tony Jordan as one of the greats like Jimmy, and I got in touch with him the night before my episode of *The Street* went out, saying how much I wanted to work with him and I told him when the episode was on. Days later I got an email from him saying he loved the episode and was putting a cop show together and asked would I be interested. It was great to be part of *Holby Blue* and working with writers like Jeff Povey, Sarah Phelps, James Payne, Richard Davidson, all names I had seen on screen, whose work I had admired and here I was now part of the same team. Working with Tony showed me just how much fun working in TV could be. He then asked me to write on *Echo Beach*, which was also a lot of fun. And you get paid too!

NG: *From a writing point of view what was the experience of writing for* Doctors*? Why did you choose to do it? What was the writing process from pitch to screen?*

MP: I've always liked the idea of a *Play for Today* type story and thought *Doctors* would be a great platform to tell some of these stories I had in mind. I also really like being part of a team on a long-running series and I was missing that after *River City*. The surprise for me was after working on *The Street*, *Holby Blue*, *Waterloo Road* and the soaps that I assumed they would take me on straight away, but I was asked to do a trial. I think part of this is to gauge your knowledge and commitment to the show. I did it, it went well and I then started pitching stories. The editor liked the story I did for the trial script, so when they found an episode that it would fit they commissioned me. It was an enjoyable process and the episode was well received. Again, the minute it went out I had emails from friends who had saw it before I had and said how touching it was. The editor said the people at *Doctors* were watching it in the office and there wasn't a dry eye, so that's nice to know you've moved someone. It was quite a poignant story about an old woman with Alzheimer's who is put into a care home and 'sprung' by her old friend who has been secretly in love with her for years. The friend was played by the fantastic Brian Cant, who has Parkinson's and who is still acting. He stole the show. It was a brilliant piece of casting and really added to the poignancy. It's the only episode I've done but I still pitch them stories.

NG: *Would it be fair to say you are a writer that prefers to tell self-contained stories, which is why you thrive on shows like* The Street *and* Moving On*? Is it also why you now have had success in feature film projects?*

MP: I like both actually. The opportunities are limited for the single stories. I pitched shows after I did *The Street* that were six self-contained stories like a *Play for Today* but all on a common theme or in a similar world, but serial drama is still the safe bet and I don't think *The Street* has changed that, which is a shame. *The Accused* fits well into that niche and it's what Jimmy is great at, so when they do come along it always makes great TV. *Moving On* is another great example of that and they do a fantastic job on a daytime budget and attract a great cast. I do like to write films, too, and am usually working on treatments for some project or other and there are people chasing the money to get me to write them. I did *Act of Grace* for the love of it, but that way of working is risky, as it's time-consuming and doesn't pay the mortgage, so I can say I've done my low-budget feature now, a bit like my graduation film. Even though we are all proud of *Act of Grace*, I've got the wisdom to pass up a project now if it looks like it'll be done on a wing and a prayer and a million favours from people with no guarantee of ever getting paid. It doesn't put me off features, though, as I've got another couple in the pipeline that are looking like they might fly, so here's hoping.

NG: *You are well-established television writer but it seems it still remains difficult to get your own authored series?*

MP: I often feel with broadcasters it's like that cheese shop sketch by Monty Python. A guy goes into a cheese shop and asks for some cheese, but the shopkeeper comes up with every excuse under the sun not to sell him any. It's easy to take it personally, and there's nothing more I'd love than to get my own series, so I keep on pitching. I don't let it get me down. You've just got to keep the faith that the right idea will happen at the right time with the right people involved.

NG: *What kind of writer do you think you're perceived as? Has that helped or hindered you?*

MP: I have been labelled the kind of writer who does the gritty stuff well, but also someone who is quite prolific. I suppose like an actor you have to have a bit of a range to get noticed. I'm currently writing a hard-hitting prison drama and loving every minute of it, but I equally love writing comedy or something poignant that will tug at the heartstrings. *The Royal* was quite gentle, so was *High Road*. *Doctors* was poignant. *Moving On* was also a moving piece. I was also asked to adapt a novel which is a mother's story about her ability to cope with her disabled baby and how this new addition affects the whole family. The producer saw my past work and knew I would do the story justice so I got hired and got to work with the amazing Paula Milne as script executive and it's a script I'm very proud of. I might not have got that if I hadn't done *The Street* and written a moving family story. In the past I've had someone say 'Oh, well you're a comedy writer, aren't you?' and it's annoying that people still make those assumptions based on one piece of work.

I have had it almost hinder me with a short film I did called *Instant Credit*. It was a comedy I did years ago. A few years later I got recommended for a comedy feature. The producer took one look at the short film and the soaps that littered my CV and instantly formed an opinion, saying this is totally different from what I've done in the past and if this is how I write comedy then I'm not suitable, or words to that effect. *Instant Credit* was one type of comedy with some bad language in it; the feature was another with no bad language in it. I then had to fight my case and give them quotes from people I'd worked with and the stuff I'd done that countered that argument. I got a crack at it and wrote the opening of the film, as I saw it. I got the gig through the writing and am now working with the same producer on something of theirs they think I am suitable for, now that they know me. The strange thing is that the subject matter is so far removed from anything I have done before, if they'd formed the same opinion of me for this without first knowing me or my range, I wouldn't be doing this with them.

NG: *What is your typical writing day?*

MP: I'm quite disciplined. You have to be. I can't spend a day messing about. If I don't write something or do meetings that move a project on, I feel like I'm skiving and I don't like that and will do double the following day to make up for it. A bit like flaying myself! I'm quite hard on myself that way and am always trying to find the right balance. On a typical day I start about nine-ish and work till the kids come in from school. I work from home mainly, so it has its good and its bad points. I like quiet when I work. If I'm on a deadline, I'll work on, sometimes till late until I've made headway. Of course I do still work on shows who are 'masters of the weekend rewrite' who will wait all week to give you notes, send them to you on a Friday and need the next draft on their desk Monday morning. It's quite common, and strangely enough becoming increasingly popular on a lot of shows! It just goes with the job.

NG: *What is the best thing about being a scriptwriter?*

MP: Seeing your work on screen and that feeling of accomplishment of having your work go out to 9 million people and having people remember what you've done, like *The Street* for example. It's great when you've done something that isn't mediocre but sticks in people's minds. You know you're doing something right then.

NG: *What is the worst thing?*

MP: The weekend rewrite or thinking you will be free of a project and because of one reason or another it doesn't go as planned and you end up having to write it on your family holiday. The amount of insane people who work in TV who quite clearly shouldn't be there but have a say over your work.

NG: *What advice would you give up new writers?*

MP: Don't look for loyalty. Be persistent. Take on board constructive criticism. Learn early on how to spot the timewasters and incompetents from the people who know what they are doing. Remain gracious and try at all times to resist the urge to leap across the table and punch someone! More importantly, have something you can fall back on, because there will be times when you will need it.

10

Storytelling techniques

In this chapter you will learn:
- *how to keep the dramatic tension high throughout a TV drama*
- *how to use plot twists to keep the audience interested*
- *how to tackle the tricky issue of exposition.*

> *Plot is: The King died and then the Queen died.*
> *Story is: The King died and then the Queen died of a broken heart.*

Dramatic tension

Dramatic tension is the embers that keep the flame of any drama smouldering, threatening to erupt into a blazing fire at any moment. It is the heart of the drama where conflict is unresolved. You will need to establish what the unresolved conflict is and create the best scenarios where that conflict turns from an ember into a flame. Inevitably, that dramatic tension as it becomes ever unbearably hotter has to ignite and the flame turns into an inferno.

This conflict has to have the potential to be divisive and painful if brought out into the open. You, as the writer, need to make the audience aware of the emotional turmoil your characters are experiencing over this conflict by conveying this through their actions and non-actions (how they avoid the issue). There has to be a reason why this conflict can't explode into the open. There has to be some straitjacket that prevents the characters from confronting the issue head on.

Take the example of the wife and the adulterous husband. What keeps that situation from being confronted? It may be that they have a young family and there is a conflict between a need to confront the truth and the need to protect the young children who love both parents. It may be because of the constraints of the social setting – a funeral, for example – where it would be inappropriate to 'make a row'.

Each scene or sequence needs to fan the flames of the secret your character or characters are keeping. The fan can evolve into a bellows that supplies so much oxygen to the flames that eventually the fire is no longer containable and the inferno is inevitable. Once that particular conflict has reached its climax, there are the inevitable consequences and another source of tension will arise.

The worst thing that can happen in drama is forgiveness. Forgiveness is like throwing water onto the embers. Unless, of course, that forgiveness is not heartfelt or provokes another source of dramatic tension, it should not be seen until the very end of the drama.

Everything happens for a reason

Everything you write in a script must be there for a reason – either to move the narrative along and/or to reveal something about character. It need not be explained in the moment but it should be explained in retrospect at the drama's end. If the story you're telling and the characters you've created are engaging, the audience will accept a degree of confusion. In some ways you are teasing the audience by saying: 'I'm not going to tell you the why or how now, but when I do you will appreciate it.' Defer the audience's gratification as much as you can about a character or storyline and reward them with a sensational reveal when the time is right.

> **'Mystery is the catalyst for imagination.'**
>
> J.J. Abrams

Plot twists

Audiences hate being cheated when some totally unexpected and unexplained event occurs to resolve a drama. You should be able to work backwards and figure out all the clever twists the writer has created and the unpredictable turn they have taken us on and it should all make sense.

There is a term in drama called 'signposting' which refers to when the audience knows exactly where something is going and is not surprised either how or when they get there. This is a disappointing experience for the viewer. The writer has to know how to surprise and utilize their craft effectively to create what are known as **plot twists**.

Plots twists, however, shouldn't come out of the blue, but need to be prepared for. Something seemingly innocuous said or shown earlier in the plot turns out to be incredibly important and affects the outcome of the story in a major way. It could be anything: a piece of information about something or someone, a prop, an idea, a character's talent. It is something that can be slipped into a conversation or displayed visually early on in the script, but its significance need not be apparent until later in the scene, the act or episode or series arc.

In Marc Pye's brilliant script 'The Flasher' for the RTS/BAFTA/ Emmy-winning drama series *The Street*, created by Jimmy McGovern, the writer seeds the resolution of his story in the inciting incident. His script tells the heartfelt story of an innocent man, Brian Peterson, who is wrongfully accused of flashing when he urinates in the bushes in a public park (see Industry interview 4).

The excerpt in Figure 10.1 is Scene 8 of the shooting script (pages 5–6) and the Inciting Incident of the drama. Buried within the scene is the resolution.

The second excerpt (Figure 10.2) is Scene 60 (pages 61–62) of the script and provides the resolution just as Brian is leaving the street.

In the first excerpt the focus is on Brian and his reaction to being confronted by Carly. This is followed by Carly's reaction and that of her father, Frannie. Brian makes a choice which makes him look like a guilty man. The Frisbee, the reason Carly was there, is overlooked but is key to the resolution. It's something innocuous but is the seed that blooms into importance at the end.

The skill is to slip the key things into the script almost unnoticed until their presence needs to be highlighted.

EXT. PARK - DAY 1

Brian, wearing tracksuit bottoms, runs along the park. He
bursts into a sprint, pushing himself, and freeing himself from
the tensions of the day. He slows down and gets his breath
back.

He needs to pee. Seeing the coast is clear, he heads off to
some nearby trees and pees. He closes his eyes and breathes a
sigh of relief. He gives his penis a couple of shakes.

A beat, and a frisbee bounces off the tree, close to his head.
Brian snaps to and turns to see a shocked looking 6yr old girl
(Carly) a few feet away. She freezes when she sees him. Her
small terrier barks at him.

Brian, realising how it must look, quickly puts his penis away,
as Carly screams and runs. The dog follows.

Brian, panicked, watches as Carly alerts her large father
(Frannie), and points in Brian's direction. Frannie looks
towards Brian, squinting to see him through the branches.

                         BRIAN
          Shit.

Brian contemplates stepping out and giving an explanation.

                        FRANNIE
                     (furious)
          Hey you, y' dirty bastard!

Brian thinks better of it and runs for his life, through the
trees, branches whipping off him and snapping, as he runs
blindly.

                       FRANNIE (O.C.)
          I'll kill you, y' dirty bastard!

A panicking Brian runs through the trees, and out of sight.
Frannie gives up the chase and heads back to the shaken Carly
and the approaching figure of a 15yr old girl who we can't
quite make out (Jenna).

Figure 10.1 'The Flasher', Scene 8, episode of The Street © ITV Granada

```
INT. THE DORAN HOUSE: LIVING ROOM - DAY 9

A concerned Liz stands at the window, watching Brian, as he
gets in the taxi.  Frannie and Jenna enter.  Jenna wipes her
eyes.  Frannie fumes and puts on his coat.  Carly puts the lead
on the dog.  Frannie composes himself and plasters a smile on
his face for Carly.

                        FRANNIE
                   (to Carly)
              You all set?

Carly nods.  Frannie takes another deep breath to calm himself.
He heads for the door and glances at the dog.

                        FRANNIE
              Where's his frisbee?

                        CARLY
              I left it in the car park.

                        FRANNIE
                   (rolls his eyes)
              Have to get him another one.  He loves
              that thing.

He goes to head through the door.

                        CARLY
              It had that man's wee on it.

Frannie stops in his tracks.  He slowly turns.  Frannie, Jenna
and Liz look at Carly, as they try to take in what she's just
said.

                        FRANNIE
              What man?

                        CARLY
                   (nods at Jenna)
              That man out there.  Her teacher.

Jenna and Liz's eyes widen.  They look to Frannie, who stands
rooted to the spot.  Carly looks at their dumb faces.

                        CARLY
              The Frisbee landed in his wee.  I
              picked it up and got some on me hand.

Carly pulls a disgusted face as she recalls.

On Frannie's realisation.
```

Figure 10.2 'The Flasher', Scene 60, episode of The Street © ITV Granada

Exposition

Exposition is information that the audience needs to know. It is the biggest bane of scriptwriters everywhere because that information must be conveyed in an accessible way without boring the audience.

Police dramas often have great swathes of exposition to deposit on the audience. Lisa Holdsworth, a writer on *New Tricks*, speaks about writing everything out and then cutting the dialogue back to its bare minimum and let the actors plough through it. Alternatively, her preferred method is to have the characters engage in banter while incidentally revealing important nuggets of information (see Industry interview 3).

In David Shore's excellent medical drama series *House*, there was a lot of medical jargon in the show but the scriptwriters utilized the differing attitudes of the characters coupled with House's own manipulations to make the necessary exposition more palatable for the audience. In this scene from an episode entitled 'The Socrates Method' (Figure 10.3), writer John Mankiewicz adds the extra dimension of the time of night.

Exposition can often be something that the characters already know and so it would be unnatural for them to discuss it. Some shows

```
INT. HOUSE'S OFFICE -- NIGHT

House and the team, called out of their sleep, and not real
happy about it.

                    FOREMAN
          Drooling, spastic movements,
          attention loss, rocking - this
          woman has classic schizophrena -

                    HOUSE
          I have a headache.  That's my only
          symptom.  I go see three doctors:
               (to Foreman)
          The neurologist says it's an
          aneurysm.
               (to Cameron)
          The immunologist says I've got hay
          fever.
               (to Chase)
          The intensivist can't be bothered,
          sends me to a shrink who tells me
          I'm punishing myself because I want
          to have sex with my mommy.

                    FOREMAN
               (pointed)
          - maybe you're just not getting
          enough sleep -

                    HOUSE
          Pick your specialist and you pick
          your disease.

House Cameron yawns, she can't help it, she's half asleep.

                    CAMERON
          This isn't about the DVT?  Or the -

                    HOUSE
               (frustrated)
          It was never about the DVT.

                    FOREMAN
          Get over to Pompeii, warn them
          about the volcano.

                    HOUSE
          If it's not schizophrenia, what
          else presents with psych symptoms?

A beat.  House is not going to get off this.
```

Figure 10.3 'The Socrates Method', episode of House © *Universal Television*

                    CAMERON
          Porphyria.

                    CHASE
          Madness of King George.

                    CAMERON
          Kuru. Beri-Beri.

                    HOUSE
          Lucy Palmero likes cheeseburgers, I
          don't think she's been eating
          brains in southeast Asia.

                    CAMERON
          The copper thing. What's it
          called? It's genetic, body
          accumulates too much copper.

                    CHASE
          Wilson's Disease.

                    HOUSE
          Very rare... Nice. I like it.

A beat.

                    FOREMAN
               (edge)
          If any of us did this, you'd fire
          us.

                    HOUSE
          Funny, I thought I encouraged you
          to question -

                    FOREMAN
          - you're not questioning. You're
          hoping. You want it to be
          Wilson's. Give her a couple of
          drugs, boom, she's okay.

House picks up Luke's book.

                    HOUSE
          June 17. Appointment with a Dr
          Karn -

                    CAMERON
          She didn't go; she didn't keep a
          single shrink appointment he made
          after -

Figure 10.3 (cont.) The Socrates Method', episode of House © Universal Television

```
                    HOUSE                        3.
        No.  Karn isn't a shrink; I looked
        it up.  He's an ophthalmologist.
        Why would she need her eyes
        checked?

                    CAMERON
               (this is thin)
        Wilson's presents with cataracts.
        I think.

                    HOUSE
        Yes, it does.  It can also cause
        the slight cirrhosis Dr. Chase so
        eagerly attributed to alcohol.  Why
        are we still here?
```

Figure 10.3 (cont.) 'The Socrates Method', episode of House © Universal Television

introduce a newbie character so stuff can be explained to both the new character and the audience at the same time.

Writing convincing exposition is often problematic but the best writers find inventive solutions. Tony Jordan, creator of *Hustle*, researched the world of the conman and knew the audience needed to know information that the characters would never discuss among themselves including the observation that 'You can't cheat an honest man. You look for someone who wants something for nothing.' Jordan's solution to this script problem was creative and had a profound effect on the show's look. Read his solution in Figure 10.4.

Other exposition can be portrayed visually without a word being spoken. Family photographs displayed on a mantelpiece or a newspaper headline or a half-seen document may be used to convey key information, for example.

Avoid long speeches – utilize banter or have something else going on that can lead to physical or verbal interjections.

Try this
▶ Watch a cop/detective show and identify all the clues that lead to the capture of the bad guy.
▶ Sketch out the storyline from beginning to end.
▶ Identify the climax and describe the resolution.
▶ Does it all make sense?
▶ Now do the same with your own storyline.

```
INT. OFFICE BLOCK.  ROOM 1205 - DAY 3.  1510
```

WILLIAMS listens intently to MICKEY as STACIE enters with tray
of coffee.

> MICKEY
> What I'm about to show you may be
> foolproof, but it's also illegal.
> There's no victim, but it's against
> the law.
>> (a beat)
> Would you like me to continue?

A moment. On WILLIAMS; Then;

Freeze the action.

Even STACIE's coffee tray is frozen in mid-air, WILLIAMS frozen
too.

MICKEY, DANNY, ALBERT and STACIE walk round to gather on edge
of desk facing camera.

ASH enters in chauffeur suit and stands with them.

They face the camera, almost like family photo shoot....

> MICKEY (CONT'D)
>> (to camera.)
> You see... The first rule of the
> con...

> STACIE
> You can't cheat an honest man.

> DANNY
> Never been done.

> ALBERT
> Can't happen.

> ASH
> Impossible.

> MICKEY
> The only way this thing works is if
> you want something for nothing.

> ASH
> So what do we do?

> STACIE
> Give you nothing for something...

Figure 10.4 'Episode title', episode of Hustle © *Kudos Film and Television*

2

> MICKEY
> (in WILLIAMS' ear;)
> You're a grand up so far.

> DANNY
> Good time to walk away.

> MICKEY
> But he can't.

> ALBERT
> Because he's greedy.

> ASH
> So what do we do?

> STACIE
> Feed the greed.

> MICKEY
> But he's got one last chance...

They move to surround WILLIAMS.

> ASH
> We've told him it's illegal.

> DANNY
> (to WILLIAMS)
> You could lose everything.

> MICKEY
> (to WILLIAMS)
> Career, wife, home...

> ALBERT
> (to WILLIAMS)
> Go to prison.

> ASH
> (to WILLIAMS)
> Get out while you can.

> STACIE
> (to WILLIAMS)
> Do the smart thing.

Everyone takes their original places, ASH leaves, DANNY and
ALBERT sit either side of WILLIAMS, MICKEY sits behind desk,
STACIE holds on to tray.

Resume action.

3

> WILLIAMS
> Hey... Laws are made to be broken...

MICKEY glances at camera.

Figure 10.4 (cont.)' Episode title', episode of Hustle © Kudos Film and Television

Key advice

▶ Keep the dramatic tension high almost to the very end.

▶ Keep your audience guessing by using surprising and inventive plot twists.

▶ Avoid being too obvious about exposition – feed the audience the information they need to know as succinctly and unobtrusively as possible.

11

The scene

In this chapter you will learn:
- *that every scene must have a clear purpose*
- *what to include in the scene heading*
- *how to write scene descriptions*
- *how to write scene action.*

Scenes are the building blocks of your story and it is very important that each scene has a purpose. The purpose of a scene has to either move the story forward or advance the plot. If a scene, no matter how well written, does not do this, it needs to be cut. Ask the question: If I take this scene out, is the script the worst for it? If there appears to be no gap in the script – then it can go.

Types of scenes

Establishing scene This is usually used to establish a location or sense of place or visual information.

Dialogue scene This is a scene that conveys information, reveals character and has conflict.

Scene sequence These are series of scenes that are linked together by a single idea.

The basics

For every scene, you need to ask yourself a few basic questions. Making these few essential decisions will help you to write the scene more effectively.

WHERE DOES IT TAKE PLACE?

The first decision you have to make about every scene is the *where* – interior or exterior, plus a location. Immediately, the writer is making a visual decision and sets the tone for the scene. If it is a police interview room or courtroom or workplace, there may be a formal atmosphere to the scene. In a park playground or changing room the atmosphere will probably be informal.

The location of the scene may be dictated by the nature of the story but if you can pick a location that is visually interesting and allows something else to be going on as well, that will add further texture to your story.

WHEN DOES IT OCCUR?

The next important decision is the *when* – when does the scene take place? Is it morning, noon or night? Is one of the characters rushing to open up the night club or to close up the shop or on the school run? An empty night club in daylight is a very different place to one at night. Visiting someone's house in the morning is different from going there early in the evening.

Whether the scene is interior or exterior, the location and the time of day together make up your **scene heading** (see Chapter 1 for more information).

WHO IS IN THE SCENE?

Who is going to populate your scene? How many characters and what is their purpose in the scene? It doesn't mean that every character in a scene has to speak to warrant their place there but they do have to be there for a reason.

WHAT IS THE SCENE ABOUT?

What is the viewer (or reader) meant to learn from the scene? Is it a piece of information that will help the investigation? Is it a piece of information that puts doubt in the mind of the wife who suspects her husband is having an affair? Does it show off a skill that a character may utilize later in the story? Be clear about what the scene is about.

You need to decide which character will drive the scene. Is it the character that wants something? Is it the character who wants to say something? Is it the character who wants to keep a secret? Through such decisions the writer creates a scene dynamic which during the course of the scene might see a shift in power from the person driving the scene to the person who is initially under the cosh.

How long should a scene be?

A scene should be as short as it possibly can. For each scene, the writer needs to cut to the chase and dispense with preamble. Go straight to the point of the scene, which means starting every scene as 'late' in the story as you possibly can. Once the scene has done its job, the scene should end straight away. Scene writing maxim: start late, finish early.

There is no hard-and-fast rule about the length of scenes per se. Some scenes can be seconds long; others can be minutes long. It all depends on your writing style and style of your show. However, generally speaking, three-page scenes are frowned upon, although everyone is free to break this rule if the scene is engaging and good.

And that is important. Each scene has to be engaging and good and make you want to move to the next scene, because if it isn't it won't matter an iota where you've set the scene, who is in it, or whether you start late or finish early.

Scene description

You have written your scene heading and now you have taken us, geographically, to the place you want the scene to play. What information do you need to include in your scene description?

As always you want to be economic with your words. You are creating an atmosphere to reflect character, so the words you use should give a sense of place and tone. The description should use broad strokes and the words should be evocative and image-oriented. Do use descriptive nouns or metaphors or similes. Don't use loads of adjectives to support a generic noun. Everything is implied. Be specific about something only if it is essential to the story.

Figures 11.1 and 11.2 are two examples of scene description from the BBC detective drama *New Tricks*. This episode, entitled 'Left Field', was written by Lisa Holdsworth. The first is the opening scene and sets up where Halford and Pullman are.

EXT. INGRAM'S HOUSE - DAY 1 1030

HALFORD and PULLMAN pull up outside a row of run down council
houses. There is litter swirling around their feet and graffiti
on the walls.

> HALFORD
> You take me to the nicest places.

> PULLMAN
> Hopefully we won't be here long, if
> this case is as open and shut as
> Strickland thinks it is.

> HALFORD
> So this bloke Ingram wants to make a
> confession twenty-five years after the
> fact. Have we spoken to his mental
> health worker?

> PULLMAN
> John Ingram does have a link to the
> missing boy. He was a friend of the
> family.

They make their way over to one of the houses.

> HALFORD
> So? What do we think? His conscience
> got the better of him?

> PULLMAN
> Maybe he got religion while he was
> inside?

She knocks at the door as...

> HALFORD
> I think there's another reason for all
> this.

> PULLMAN
> What?

As if to answer her two HOODIES come flying past on a BMX bike.
The one standing on the back wheel axle throws something as...

> HOODY 1
> Dirty paedo!

> HALFORD
> Well, for a start, the local wildlife
> leaves something to be...

Figure 11.1 'Left Field', Scene 1, episode of New Tricks © Wall To Wall

```
However, he turns to see that Pullman has taken a raw egg to
her chest. The yolk is still dripping from her coat.

                          PULLMAN
                     (steaming)
                Wait here.

As she goes to the car, the door opens and Ingram (50s, slight,
haunted) pokes his head out.

                          INGRAM
                Are you Detective Superintendent
                Pullman?

There is a screech of tyres as Pullman drives after the
hoodies.

                          HALFORD
                She'll be back in a minute. She's just
                doing a bit of community policing.
```

Figure 11.1 (cont.) '*Left Field*', *Scene 1, episode of* New Tricks © Wall To Wall

The second is in an interior scene in the living room of the suspect, Anne. Note how the description tells us about the character.

This visual image is far superior to any description Halford could make of the house to a colleague. The viewer makes their own judgement as to what type of character Anne is.

INT. ANNE'S HOUSE. LIVING ROOM - DAY 1 1450

ANNE (50s, bright, passionate, pragmatic) shows Pullman and
Standing into her cluttered but tidy front room. The shelves
are full, ceiling to floor, with books. In amongst the tomes
are classy souveniers from foreign travel. Over the mantelpiece
is Banksyesque canvas which shows a helmeted bobby and several
CCTV and speed cameras staring out of the canvas. Standing
raises an eyebrow at this as...

                    ANNE
          Yes, I had a phone call from DAC
          Strickland. He told me that Ingram had
          finally done the right thing.

                    PULLMAN
          Finally?

                    ANNE
          Well, it was all fairly obvious once
          we found out about his history. He
          lived locally and he'd been to
          meetings in our home. Yasser knew him
          and must have trusted him enough to go
          with him. And after Yasser was gone we
          never heard from Ingram again. It just
          makes sense. Doesn't it?

Standing is noting the titles of some of the books on Anne's
shelves.

                    PULLMAN
          We still have to do a proper
          investigation...

                    STANDING
          But you won't have a problem with
          that, will you?
               (reading the titles)
          "Miscarriages of British Justice".
          "Rough Justice in Modern Britain".
          "Are We Living in a Police State?"

                    ANNE
          I work for a civil liberties campaign
          group. It's where the real battle lies
          now. The day is coming when we won't
          be able to go anywhere, meet anyone,
          say anything without it being observed
          and noted by those in power. CCTV,
          internet monitoring, illegal phone
          taps...

Figure 11.2 'Left Field', Scene 7, episode of New Tricks © Wall To Wall

> STANDING
> But if you're doing nothing wrong,
> you've nothing to worry about have
> you?

> ANNE
> Depends who decides what is right or
> wrong. The elected government? The
> press? The military?

> PULLMAN
> Still, if there had been CCTV on
> Westminster Bridge when Yasser was
> taken.

> ANNE
> I'm aware of the double-edged sword.
> But perhaps if my son's disappearance
> had been properly investigated in the
> first place.

> PULLMAN
> You don't think it was?

> ANNE
> I think that you let the press do your
> job for you the first time around.
> Trial by journalism. The papers
> decided that myself and Fred were
> guilty of neglect. And that was that.

> PULLMAN
> Well, there'll be no press involvement
> this time. But we will need you and
> your husband's cooperation.

> ANNE
> Ex-husband. Fred and I split after...
> After Yasser.

> PULLMAN
> I'm sorry to hear that.

> ANNE
> We'd been on different paths for a
> long time. Emotionally and
> politically.

Standing and Pullman exchange a look.

Figure 11.2 (cont.) 'Left Field', Scene 7, episode of New Tricks © Wall To Wall

Scene action

Any scene action has to be conveyed with clarity and be an essential part of the story. It is important to say what you mean to help paint a moving picture in the mind's eye of the reader and express your intention to the director, though without going to the extent of suggesting camera angles!

Don't direct on the page

Avoid including camera angles, editing directions or parentheticals for speech:

Camera angles are the territory of the director and he or she will to a man and woman ignore such explicit direction from a writer. So take out all those CLOSE-UPS and PANS ACROSS. However, you *can* influence the director without resorting to camera directions. Instead of CLOSE-UP, write the reaction you want: e.g. 'JOHN grimaces' or 'MARY smiles'. Such indications express to the director that the character's reactions are important and that they will need to show them.

Editing directions (known as transitions) include instructions such as CUT TO. As a rule, avoid using these, or use them only sparingly and for impact. The reader will know there is a scene change because of the scene heading.

Parentheticals are used to tell the actor how to say a particular line. In the vast majority of cases, they are simply not needed. The way the scene is set up and the exchange of dialogue should make it clear how the line is to be delivered. Only in the rare circumstance where a line is truly ambiguous, and could thus be delivered in one of several ways, should parentheticals be used.

When writing scene action, you might find a using a thesaurus helpful so that you select the right word. For example, anyone can *walk* into a room – here 'walk' is almost a non-word because it conveys something that is everyday and bland. Look at alternatives and see if there is something better that can reveal something about a character's state of mind and/or intent. A character could step, tread, pace, stride, strut, stalk, prance, tiptoe, skip, lumber, stamp, goosestep, patter, lurch, toddle, stagger, reel, waddle, shuffle, dawdle, trudge, stomp, ambulate, perambulate, march, etc. Each word expresses a different shade of the verb 'to walk' and conveys something about your character. Consider every piece of action that you write because it is action that reveals the truth.

You may write scenes that don't have any dialogue at all, but which are action-packed with a chase or a fight. Again, think about the words you use to describe those actions and the effect that they will convey.

Tips for writing scene description and action

- ▶ With action- and/or description-heavy scenes, it is wise not to write a block of uninterrupted prose. Restrict each paragraph to no more than **four lines** before either interrupting with dialogue or another sequence of action.
- ▶ Regard each new paragraph as a cut – **a new shot.** With that you can give pace and impact to the scene and tell the reader that a character's emotional reaction or action is important.
- ▶ Try to write all scene action/description in the **present tense**. Remember you are telling a story of moving pictures so include movement – show your characters doing things. It helps keeper the reader in the moment. Once you give an instruction or attempt to explain something in the scene description, you will take the reader out of your story and you will lose the momentum and atmosphere you have worked so hard to create.

Key advice

▶ If a scene does not advance the story in any way, drop it.

▶ Make sure scene descriptions are short but evocative of the mood you want for the scene.

▶ Don't try to do the director's job in the script by including indications for camera angles and close-ups.

▶ Make sure that the scene action is punchy but evocative of character – remember, actions tell the truth.

Industry interview 5: scriptwriter (III)

Tony Jordan is one of the UK's leading scriptwriters. From his beginnings as the perceived authentic voice of EastEnders, *he went on to develop his own shows including* City Central, Holby Blue, Hustle, Life on Mars, Moving Wallpaper, Echo Beach *and* The Nativity. *He is a generous supporter of new talent through his own production company Red Planet Pictures, which also runs an annual scriptwriting contest – the Red Planet Prize.*

Nicholas Gibbs: *How did you break into television? You were famously a stallholder.*

Tony Jordan: I was working on the markets and my next-door neighbour, Doug, was a wannabe writer. He was writing scripts, sending them off and trying to get a start. I was intrigued by that – it was like he had a hobby that I didn't have. At his suggestion, I wrote a script but put in a drawer for a year until Doug told me to send it off. I didn't know where to send it, so I just put it in a big manila envelope and wrote 'BBC, London' on it and posted it. I didn't hear anything; I didn't expect to. Then about three months later I got a card from the BBC saying someone had read my script, they really enjoyed it and did I want to come in for a chat? So I went to the Script Unit had a few chats, went to a couple of seminars with John Sullivan and Carla Lane, and listened to them. I didn't want to be a writer particularly but it was a day out. The Head of the Script Unit sent the script to the producer of *EastEnders* and I got offered the job. It was that easy. So I didn't do the whole starving with the naked light bulb in a lonely room kind of thing!

NG: *Is it true that they thought you were a Londoner and you were the authentic voice of the East End?*

TJ: Oh true, that was completely true. They heard I was a market trader so I think I was sold to them as the real deal. That's may be why I got in so quick because I think they had a bit of stick about the authenticity of the real East End. East Enders weren't miserable; they were all happy and 'cor blimey, leave it out'! So I think I was sold to the producers as the real deal as the barrow boy. That turned into an East End barrow boy as obviously I would be because that's the only kind of barrow boy. So I played the part; I just did my best Dick Van Dyke impression! I knew why I was there. I wasn't a kid. I wasn't stupid. I knew what they thought I was and I went in and I played the part.

NG: *So how long did that persist? When did the truth come out?*

TJ: I think a couple of years. It was during that period everybody looked at me – I thought it was hilarious – as the oracle as to whether something was real or not. I've never lived in the East End in my life. People would turn to me at Story Table and ask: 'Would that happen in the East End, Tone?' I'd say: 'Yeah, yeah absolutely.' Then the press office called and one of the papers or a magazine or something wanted to do a feature on me growing up in the East End. I thought: 'Well, I'm going to have to come clean.' I said 'I don't know; I wasn't brought up in the East End.' Shocked silence on the end of the phone when I told them I was born in Southport on Merseyside.

NG: *You were associated with* EastEnders *for a long time. For someone who fell into it by accident did you have any stories you wanted to tell?*

TJ: No, not really. When I was writing for *EastEnders* I wasn't a writer. I didn't think of myself as a writer. I was just working on *EastEnders* doing the scripts. That's how I saw it because I never had any aspirations to be a writer. I was never a frustrated writer, I was a market trader and I was quite happy. So my feeling was never about 'I've got stories I'm longing to tell.' It was more about I know people because, even though I was not an East End barrow boy, I was a market trader surrounded by people. I talked to people, real people who came to a market on Saturday morning to buy their veg. I talked to them every day of my life so I knew how people talked to each other. I knew how funny people were. I knew how loving people could be. I knew how cruel people could be. So I wrote people properly. Not that no one else did but my episodes became, in my head, less about the storyline I had been given to do by *EastEnders* and more about Pauline and Arthur sitting in a pub talking about their marriage or the Mitchell brothers talking about 'birds'.

NG: *Your first authored series was* City Central. *How did that come about?*

TJ: I think *City Central* was the moment when I became a writer, a proper writer, whatever that means. I still don't know what that means! I spent a lot of time sitting in story meetings on other shows and rocking the boat a bit saying 'Why don't we do this? Should we do it this way? Can we do that? Why do you do it that way?' I didn't know any better but to question everything. The way I wrote as well would ignore storylines and people would say 'You haven't done this.' And I'd say: 'Yeah, I know but I had loads of fun doing this karaoke competition instead.' So *City Central* was the first time I was in control. I could create the characters, I could create the world, and I could create the stories. It was like, 'Wow, I haven't got to convince anybody now so I just have to convince myself.' I loved it and it is probably one of the things I'm most proud of – still.

NG: *You wrote most of the episodes on* City Central *but not all and you brought other writers in...*

TJ: You have to. It happens on every show because it's not possible.

NG: *Is it hard to hand over your characters to someone else?*

TJ: No, not at all. It's like being a kid and getting a really cool bike. I remember getting my first Raleigh Chopper and it was great but then my mates didn't have one. I loved to say to them 'Get on and have a go because it's brilliant.' I think like that with most of my other shows. I think it is brilliant to see what other people do with my characters and so I love it.

NG: *Do you give those writers a free rein or is there an element of prescription with storylines?*

TJ: It kind of depends on what it is. There's no restriction on storylines. I used to do storylining because I was doing that on *EastEnders*. I'd do some but the best writers ignore some of that like I had done. They've dumped it, done their own thing and you get an episode that is completely brilliant. Some writers came and stuck slavishly to what I did, what I'd said and my ideas and it wasn't quite as great. You need to have balls as a writer. On *City Central* it was a bit of both. It was a good experience.

NG: *After Series 3 when* City Central *wasn't recommissioned, were you disappointed or did you think it had come to the end of its natural life?*

TJ: I kind of did two series of *City Central*. They brought in another writer to come and showrun it. I lost a little bit of love for *City Central* after two series and I don't know why. I think by then people were starting to give me notes and I felt people were trying to change it from what I wanted it to be. So it carried on and I didn't really have a lot to do with the third series if I'm honest.

NG: *Was it a question of having pressure from above about what the show should be but you having your own vision of what it should be?*

TJ: You always get pressure because someone has given you the money to make it. It can be your show. I've even got it now. *Hustle*'s my show. It's going out on someone else's channel and they have their own agenda about what they want their channel to portray, what they want on their channel, what they want to spend their money on. They've got all those things to worry about and I completely get it. It's not a bad thing. I've been really lucky that creatively I haven't had too many people trying to change what I want to do.

NG: *What about* Holby Blue *because that was a show that was generated from an existing franchise?*

TJ: That was really interesting for me. A lot of people were surprised that I did something like *Holby Blue* because I'd never written *Holby* or *Casualty*. I haven't got anything against them; I just never had a feeling that it was my kind of thing. I liked the fact that people are surprised with everything I've done. People in the media love you to be something. They love you to be a really serious drama writer or a lighter drama writer. They love you to be a comedy writer or a drama writer or a movie writer or a sitcom writer. I think I want to be all those things. I just think if you write, write. I get a kick out of the fact I've written *Moving Wallpaper* and *The Nativity*. That makes me laugh. So the fact that people were asking why was I doing *Holby* made me want to do it all the more. I thought: 'Wow, this is really cool.' I created *Holby Blue*, created characters and just did what I do really. I loved *Holby Blue*; I thought it was a great show. I formed my production company to make *Holby Blue*. I was looking for the right project to produce. So making that step into production with *Holby Blue* seemed a really good idea.

NG: *Why did* Holby Blue *come to an end?*

TJ: It would still be going now but what happened was we had a change of BBC1 controller. Whereas the controller who had ordered it thought it was great that there were all these linked series; the new controller who came in thought there shouldn't be so many of these shows, particularly linked together in that way. Neither of those two controllers was right and neither of those controllers was wrong; it's just the way the world is.

NG: *When* Hustle *first hit the screens it was so different not just in writing but in the way it looked. Was that all down to you?*

TJ: Yes, I think so. *Hustle* looked so beautiful, so classy, had such high production values with sexy, cool London, because of the director Bharat Nalluri and executive producer Jane Featherstone and Kudos, the company that made it. The other stuff: the freeze frames and the trickery things and the talking to camera and all that stuff were things that I did because they were solutions to problems I had when I was writing the script. I'd read about 30 books on cons and I knew all this information about how cons worked, about the sequence of events and why you did things in a certain way but the audience didn't. I found characters were having huge chunks of dialogue – exposition – explaining what was going on. I thought: 'This is terrible but I need to get this information across. I need to find another way of doing it.' So basically I created all those things to stop it being naff. Instead of one character saying to another 'You can't cheat an honest man. You look for someone who wants something for nothing.' If I wrote that, it would have been naff if one character said it to another. Why would they have that conversation? Don't they know that? They're both conmen but I want the audience to know that. So I thought I'll get one of my characters to tell the audience. I wrote the freeze frame and all the characters came to the front and sat on the desk and did their little speech and then went back to live action and I developed things from there. That's why my characters talk to camera; that's why we did the freeze frame things. So all those things were solutions to problems I had writing the script.

NG: *Did you see it as a big risk when no one else was doing it?*

TJ: None of these things are risks. There's no such thing as risk in television. It is only a risk if you know what will be a hit. If you look over the edge of a ravine and there is an eight-foot gap, you know if you fall down that ravine you will be smashed to smithereens. You will be dead. Therefore, jumping that gap is a risk because you understand the nature of the problem. The thing with television is I don't know what the risk is because I don't know what will happen. I don't know what works, I don't know what doesn't. Instinctively, within an episode I might know what works and what doesn't and what's funny and what isn't, but I might be wrong about that as well. As to whether an audience will love the idea of a series or the way it's shot – I don't know. I don't know of any manual that says this is how to make a guaranteed hit series.

NG: *Broadcasters have a perception of risk because they provide the money?*

TJ: They have that for very good particular reasons. That's their agenda and it has nothing to do with creativity. I deal in the creative world. The BBC has an agenda. The agenda is that they have to be careful about what they put on screen and what criticism that may attract and for what reason. They have to be seen to be spending the money on things which are for the public good. The reason they have that agenda is because of the licence fee; they're a public service. So they are absolutely right to have that. I can't have those things. I'm not a public service. I'm trying to tell the best story that I can tell. So sometimes when we're in meetings there is a conflict between those two different things.

I've just been talking to the BBC about the best script I've ever written, which is about a guy who sells his soul to the devil; I think it is best thing I've written and they've just turned it down. They turned it down because they said they don't think they can show this on the BBC. And do you know what? I agree with them. I think they are probably right but that's fine, that's cool. I'm not going to change the script. ITV have got an agenda because they have got their advertisers and they want bums on seats because bums on seats equals revenue, which means the channel can stay alive and everyone gets paid at the end of the week. I get that. So if I dream up something that is a bit off the wall, a bit strange or a bit weird, something that three men and a dog are going to want to see, they may turn it down. But that is their agenda. Until I have got my own channel I don't have to worry about that stuff; I just have to get a story and then find the right home for it. Sometimes the right home is in my bottom drawer because it will never be made in the way I think it should be made.

NG: *You did eight successful seasons of* Hustle. *Why did it end?*

TJ: I think it was fuelled by me saying 'I've think I've done my *Hustle*.' It was tougher and tougher for me to do and also the biggest thing was that I was aware that I wasn't going to hold on to my cast. They were all out of contract after Series 7. We said we wanted to do one more. We got them all back but you're not going to hold on to Adrian Lester, Robert Glenister and Robert Vaughn. That's never going to happen, so you're never going to have that. So as we were talking about Series 8 I knew we had a choice: we could either lose a couple but I'd have to replace Adrian with someone else and Robert Glenister, who, for me, has always been the rock around which everything else is built. It's not going to be *Hustle* anymore. Or I thought should we just go out in a blaze of glory with Robert Vaughan as Albert Stroller. So that was it really. Jane Featherstone, who I started *Hustle* with, agreed and so we said Series 8 would be the last.

NG: *Is it still generally the case you get more noes than yeses?*

TJ: Oh yes, completely. You look at all the drama slots and you look at all the drama writers from all over the world; basically, they are all vying for those slots. There will be a lot of noes. I've taken enough projects to the broadcasters that would fill all the slots. They've got to say no to someone. You hope the best ones get picked up and they turn down the worst ones.

NG: *You are philosophical about the fate of your scripts then?*

TJ: What am I going to do about it? I don't live in a world where I've got people queuing up outside Red Planet waiting to shoot every word that I write. I do what everyone else does. I get an idea, I pitch it. Sometimes it gets picked up; sometimes it's bought and sometimes it's not.

NG: *How did the Red Planet Prize come about?*

TJ: I was talking to a writer called Danny Stack. We were having a coffee and we were talking about Red Planet and he said I should do a writing competition and I thought yes I should. I dislike writers who get a break and pull the ladder up and shut the door behind them. There are a lot of those about and I just think it's a shame. Drama in this country is written by the same 12 old farts – and I include myself in that – you've got to have new blood coming through. You need the next generation of writers, so that was the idea really. The Red Planet Prize is to find the next generation of writers.

NG: *You are one of the few indies who accept unsolicited material. You must be inundated?*

TJ: I get told off all the time by my people in Red Planet because it puts so much pressure on to the company to deal with it. Sometimes it backfires because you can't read it as quickly as we want to read it and people get pissed off. You think: 'What's worse? Saying no we don't want to read it or saying yes we will try and read it and then taking six months?' We do the best we can. We try and make it manageable by asking for the first ten pages. It is easier to read the first ten pages than read a whole script, so we can get through more. I know whether you can write within ten pages. I mean some bigger companies would struggle to get through what we do but it's an ideological thing with us. We're a creative company. We love writers. We love making good telly. We don't get involved in politics. We don't play games. We don't do people down. We don't nick people's ideas. We don't do any of that; we just do the best that we can do.

NG: *With* Death in Paradise *do you think that would have been made if you weren't attached to it?*

TJ: No. No, because I was a goalkeeper. Red Planet was able to say to the BBC, if it all goes wrong and if Robert can't do this and if the scripts don't work, don't worry, I will step in and fix them. They needed that reassurance but Robert was fine – he wrote the scripts and got a second series. It's on the front: created and written by Robert Thorogood. It doesn't say created and written by Robert Thorogood and Tony Jordan. It is his show; he's written the scripts. I'm at the end – it's my company and I'm executive producer.

NG: *So do you think new writers need someone like you?*

TJ: I think it helps. It's tough. I am helping with the mentoring scheme and we do the competition. I'm trying to help. You get other writers who get given their break on named writers' shows knowing they are going to be rewritten. That's a given. Whatever you write, it can be absolutely genius, but the deal is it gets overwritten by our star writer. I think that's disrespectful – it's dishonest, it's wrong. I don't mind rewriting other writers because sometimes you need to. Either they can't do it or they drop out or they're on the verge of a nervous breakdown and you're shooting in two days: they are not going to get there and need some help. But to say you just do my first draft and then I come in, swish my cape to one side and give it a little flourish of pixie dust because I'm a genius. Well, you know what, piss off! Why don't *you* do the blank page bit? *You* do the work!

NG: *Do you get broadcasters phoning you up and saying 'Tony, we're looking for a new cop series or vet series – have you got anything?'? Does that work for you?*

TJ: Briefs aren't my thing, I hate those briefs. I don't go to the broadcasters' briefs. I don't know how that works really. I much rather have a good idea then go find a channel for it. That's the best way round, I think.

NG: *How do you get people interested?*

TJ: First of all you need to understand why it's tough and I understand it completely. If a broadcaster is investing £5 million in you to make a series, they kind of want a safe pair of hands. That's all it is. It's not a bad thing. I understand that, I get it. I also understand that if they commission a series from Jimmy McGovern and it bombs that executive can say: 'How was I to know? It's Jimmy McGovern.' Whereas he orders a new series from John Doe or John Smith who no one has ever heard of and it bombs people will say to the executive: 'Why the hell did you commission that from him? Why didn't you get Jimmy McGovern?' It's not a conspiracy. It is just people watching their arses like they do in every industry, so it is not necessarily a bad thing.

NG: *What about agents?*

TJ: All I can say to you is that writers generally think they need an agent. My agent has never helped me write the words. The job needs an agent but you need an agent to get a job. You don't need an agent not to get a job. I know some people won't read your submission unless it comes from an agent. They're not going to read it anyway. Basically, what you need to do is write. The clue is in the title. You're a writer – just write. Write what you want to write with your voice. Write what makes you laugh, write what makes you scared, write what makes you cry and write your stuff. Do your voice, keep writing and write spec scripts. Still now, I write spec scripts. I can phone somebody up. I know some people will say yes; of course they will. I write spec scripts because I have freedom. I have no master because I write the scripts I want to write. You should be at home in your underpants growing a beard writing scripts, end of story. If you do that and you write scripts and keep writing and write with passion and your voice, I believe talent will out. I believe you will get there. I also think that's the only way to do it really.

NG: *What advice you can give to writers on the business of writing?*

TJ: As a general rule, try and hit your deadlines if you can. More importantly, try and believe in what you're sending in and not another piece of crap and hoping it'll be all right. Be nice to everybody, that's the most important thing. The number of writers who are rude to the script editor – I can't believe how stupid they are! The script editor they scream at as being incompetent and who has no right to be in the same room as they are because they're a genius might be controller of BBC1 one day.

12

Writer's block

In this chapter you will learn:
* *how you can overcome writer's block*.

Writer's block is the situation where you, the writer, have come to a halt because you can't think of anything to put down on the page. Here are some suggestions on how to deal with writer's block:

▶ Always stop writing when you still have something left to write but you know what is going to happen – your own writer's cliffhanger, if you like. This will mean that, when you sit down for your next writing session, you can go straight into the writing and have had the benefit of thinking about the next phase.

▶ Do something else. Play music, watch TV, read a book, play with the kids, go for a run – anything that relaxes you.

▶ Go somewhere else. A change of scenery can work wonders. Some writers go to public places like coffee shops or the local park or the pub.

▶ Write out of sequence. If you don't know what happens next, write another scene that takes place later in the story. Look at your plan, if you've made one, and see where you can go.

▶ Re-read the script. Writer's block can sometimes occur because there is a problem earlier in the script.

It is worth noting that writers tend not to get writer's block when a deadline is looming. They always find a way of getting something down on the page when there's a limited time available to them.

Key advice

▶ If you get writer's block, don't panic! It's usually just a blip.
▶ Take a break, do something else, go somewhere else.

13

The outline

In this chapter you will learn:
- *how you can use an outline to clarify your ideas*
- *how, by successively honing down your outline, you can produce an effective synopsis, pitch and logline.*

Once you've created the premise, characters, world and plots, and before you sit down to write the script proper, take your idea and write out the story in outline form, almost as if it's a short story. Follow the procedure below:

1 In the first instance splurge it all out, so everything is on paper in note form. Look at your notes, then rearrange them into a cohesive narrative order.

2 From those notes write your story in prose form, putting in as much detail as possible including the major plot points and act breaks. Using the four- or five-act structure, break down the prose into mini-chapters and cover all of the storylines. Split the prose into the constituent storylines to ensure that each makes sense as a stand-alone story. Write everything in the present tense and include any important pieces of dialogue.

3 Rewrite this synopsis as many times as you need to until everything makes sense, but limit yourself to no more than 20 pages.

4 Rewrite the story as before but now only in ten pages.

5 Rewrite the story as before but now only in five pages.

6 Rewrite the story as before but now on a single page.

7 Rewrite the story into a single paragraph (this is your pitch!)

8 Rewrite the story into a single sentence – this should match or create a better version of your logline.

This exercise thus provides you with:

▶ a **story document** to which you can refer when writing the actual script
▶ a brief, single-page **synopsis**
▶ a **pitch** that you may want to include in your covering letter to a production company
▶ a solid **logline**.

Armed with these documents, you can now write the actual script. But remember, you have to finish the script however long it takes. The first draft doesn't have to be right; it just has to be finished.

Key advice

▶ Don't start writing your script straight away – write an outline to help you ease yourself into the project and to get to its dramatic and emotional heart
▶ When you start writing the actual script, don't get too hung up on perfection. This is your first draft and the aim, at this stage, is just to get to the end!

14

....

Rewriting

In this chapter you will learn:
- *the importance of re-reading your script, looking at a different focus each time*
- *how to rewrite your script*
- *how to respond to feedback notes.*

Look at your script from every angle

Once you've finished your script, put it away for at least a couple of weeks. Don't look at it. Don't think about it. After a holiday away from your script, return and read it, then re-read it again. This time go through a series of sweeps, each of which will look at a particular aspect of the script.

CHARACTERS

Work through your cast of characters one by one and follow their through-line and ask:

▶ Does their particular storyline make sense for them?
▶ Do they act consistently throughout?
▶ Do they act naturally or do they act just to serve the plot?
▶ Check their dialogue: Is their vocabulary and sentence structure distinctive? Do they sound like anyone else in the script?
▶ Is your protagonist proactive enough?
▶ Does a character change their behaviour? If so, is there a plausible catalyst for that change?

SCENES

Go through the script scene by scene and answer these questions:

- ▶ Does the scene start as late as possible?
- ▶ Does the scene finish as early as possible?
- ▶ Does the scene move the story forward?
- ▶ Is the scene visual? That is, does it show rather than tell?
- ▶ Does the scene follow on logically from the previous scene and move on logically to the next one?
- ▶ Is there conflict within the scene?
- ▶ Has that conflict been maximized?
- ▶ Does it change the direction of the story?
- ▶ If you took the scene out of the script, would the script still make sense? If it does, cut the scene.

ACTION

Go through the script and read only the scene action, then ask yourself:

- ▶ Does the story make sense visually?
- ▶ Is the script visually interesting?
- ▶ Is the script visually dramatic?

STRUCTURE

Read the script and ask yourself the following:

- ▶ Does the script grab the audience from the beginning on an emotional level?
- ▶ Are their sufficient and regular hooks?
- ▶ Does the script surprise in its storytelling? (Have you seen something like it before? Is it too predictable?)
- ▶ Do you have a strong and satisfying ending?
- ▶ Have all the major conflicts been resolved?

More questions

Here are some more questions you should be asking as you re-read your script. The answers should come from the script in front of you, not from the idea of your story in your head:

- ▶ Is the premise set up properly? Can it be understood?
- ▶ Does the narrative flow? Is it an easy or difficult read?

- ▶ What is going on? Do you understand and run with the story?
- ▶ Is the story the one you wanted to write?
- ▶ Do the events of the narrative reflect the script's theme?
- ▶ Are there scenes, sequences or dialogue that do not relate to your central story or theme?
- ▶ What is your protagonist's goal?
- ▶ Does your protagonist and their goal drive the story? Does their progression make sense?
- ▶ Does your antagonist have a dominant enough role?
- ▶ Is the story told in a televisual fashion?
- ▶ Could any of the scenes or the storytelling be better?
- ▶ Are there any unnecessary elements in the script? A healthy script is a lean script.
- ▶ Is there too much detail?
- ▶ Does your story fulfil the expectations of the genre?

Now rewrite… and rewrite

As you go through all these questions, your answers will generate a desire to revise and rewrite. The purpose of the rewrite is to make your script better. Ultimately, someone you've probably never met will have to read this script and make a judgement on it. You want to impress that stranger, so you need the script to be the best it can be.

You will have to be tough on yourself and tough on the writing. You may have the best scene you've ever written but, if it doesn't sit well in the script because it doesn't push the story along, then cut it. If a scene isn't working, rewrite it or reposition it. It may need to be supported by additional scenes.

Now go through the script word by word:

- ▶ cut
- ▶ rewrite
- ▶ polish.

Once you've revised the script, put it away for a week and then return to it and go through the same process again.

You can revise as many times as you like but don't slip into a permanent cycle of rewriting just for the sake of it. It will serve no purpose. In fact, it could end up being the reason why your script never sees the light of day.

Script feedback

Once you are happy with your revised script, it is now time to hand your script over to trusted people who will give you feedback. You want people who will be honest with you and who understand scripts. They may be fellow writers or actors or script editors or script readers but whoever it is – and you may want to pass the script to more than one person – you must be able to trust their opinion and integrity to give an honest appraisal.

There are a number of individuals and organizations who provide a script feedback service for a fee. The services they supply can vary from a simple written report on your script to more thorough advice possibly supported by one-to-one discussion. These independent eyes are valuable for an assessment of your script.

Do your homework about any service you pay for because the fees can be quite expensive and for the money you pay you want good-quality feedback. Ask for the individual's or company's credentials. Does the reader have industry experience? How long has the company been established? What are their success stories in the marketplace? Make sure you can verify the claims. Understand exactly what you are paying for and what you can expect.

Talk to other writers and see if they can recommend any particular script feedback service. Do not balk over the fees – just make sure the fee is worthwhile. If you don't invest in yourself, why should anyone else invest in you? See the 'Taking it further' section at the end of this book for further information about script reading services.

FEEDBACK NOTES – ROUND ONE

Notes are part and parcel of the scriptwriter's lot. Even when you have achieved your goal of a script commission, there will be notes on your script from various sources and invariably delivered to you by your assigned script editor (UK) or showrunner (US).

Remember: you are asking and/or paying for an honest appraisal of your script. Do not take the report or notes as personal criticism. You want to make your script better.

Sit down with a coffee (or other favourite beverage) and read the feedback notes. Then read them again with the script by your side. Go through the script and look at the notes. It will be clear that some things in the script will need addressing (this is especially true if more than one person highlights the same thing). It will be your job as the writer to choose *how* to address the issues raised: which changes need to be made? You may decide to embrace every note or choose to ignore some if you don't agree with them. Both standpoints are equally valid. Remember: you are looking to improve your script. Not every note will be a good one and you will have to learn between the good and the bad (though the vast majority will be good).

FEEDBACK NOTES – ROUND TWO

Once you have rewritten your script in the context of the feedback received, it may be wise to go for a second round of feedback. Once again, pay attention to the notes and again address any issues. If you're getting the same note as you did from the first round of feedback, then the likelihood is it will be an issue that you will have to address – so do so.

After the latest rewrite, see if you can have the script read aloud so you can hear what it *sounds* like. Check out any local acting groups who may be able to help you. Do not participate in the read-through – just sit, listen and make notes.

Finally...

Do another final polish of the script and then a proofread. Remember: you are a writer and the tools of your trade are words – make sure they are spelled correctly and you have used the right ones.

The essence of spec scriptwriting is to get it right. Generally speaking, you do not have to rush. You are writing a script to impress. There are exceptions, of course – if, for example, you are writing a script to submit to a competition. Deadlines are important to television and being able to write quickly and under pressure is a great asset and something you are going have to do. Not only do you have to write and rewrite a script within a given timeframe, the writing has to be of the highest quality. You will only learn the quality test by writing your specs.

Do-it-yourself checks

Here is a checklist of common mistakes to look out for in your script. Do take the time to make sure everything on this list is right.

Typos   You are a writer, your tools of the trade are words and you should not be misspelling them. It never looks good.

Secondary characters   Make sure they are involved where they should be and that they do not simply drift in and out.

Time   Unless it is a time travel story, make sure time passes in a believable and realistic way.

Circumstances   Make sure every aspect of the dramatic situation has a ring of truth to it.

Dialogue   Make sure your characters sound distinctive and different from one another.

Intent   Be clear about the story you're telling. Is it the story you meant to tell? Is it the genre you intended? Are the characters right and/or consistent?

Exposition   Remember: show, don't tell.

Storytelling   Make sure the script is primarily visual – remember the medium that you're writing for.

Don't direct There should be absolutely no camera angles!

Key advice

▶ Try to read your own work as objectively as possible – using checklists like the ones in this chapter will help you keep focused on the nuts and bolts.

▶ Don't take a script reader's criticism personally – their goal and yours is to improve the script.

▶ Don't rewrite for ever – learn to know when your script is good enough to go out into the big, wide world.

Industry interview 6: the scriptwriter (IV)

Sally Wainwright is one of the UK's most successful scriptwriters and has been the creator and writer of an impressive list of original drama for both BBC and ITV. Her breakthrough series was At Home with the Braithwaites, *which ran for four seasons. Since then Sally has written a diverse range of shows such as* Jane Hall *and* The Amazing Mrs Pritchard *to the Royal Television Society award-winning drama serial* Unforgiven. *Her female detective show* Scott & Bailey *has completed a second series on ITV in 2012 and on the BBC her drama* Last Tango in Halifax *also debuted in the same year.*

Nicholas Gibbs: *You are one of the nation's top writers, by which I mean you are getting regular commissions of original work. How did you break into television?*

Sally Wainwright: Well, I started writing dialogue when I was about 11. I wrote plays for me and my sister all the time and when I got to university I wrote my first full-length stage play. I was allowed to submit it as part of my degree. I had to do a performance of it and I took it to the Edinburgh Festival. I asked as many people from the world of television as I knew, which wasn't many, but I invited everyone and I invited some agents, but nobody came at all. One agent said, 'I can't come but can you send me a copy of the script?' and she became my first agent and she sent that out to people as a calling card and it was through that I got *The Archers* when I was about 24.

NG: The Archers *is a BBC Radio 4 soap. Did you listen to the show?*

SW: I hadn't in fact. I'd heard it because my mum was a very keen listener which was really amazing for me because I'd always heard it in the background but I never followed it. It just washed straight over me. My mum was able to give me a crash course and she was so excited about me getting the chance to do it. I absorbed so much information from her very quickly. I was given a trial script and I made that work.

They offered a week's work and a contract. From that my *Archers* scripts became calling cards for other things, and I left to write *Emmerdale*, which didn't work out. I only wrote six episodes. I didn't like it and it was my early introduction to television and it was awful... it was terrible. It was all I wanted to do since I was 13 and my first introduction to it was appalling and my agent said, 'Get used to it because this is what it's like.' For me it has been the only time it has been like that.

NG: *Did that initial first bad experience of television put you off?*

SW: No, it didn't because I knew I wanted to write telly. I knew it was a crap programme so that wasn't going to put me off. The reason I had confidence in myself was at the time I had a similar approach from Granada to work on daytime soaps like *Families*. It was brilliant because you were working with people like Kay Mellor and Peter Whalley and some fantastic writers. My ultimate ambition since the age of 13 had been to write for *Coronation Street* and the fact I got a foot in the door at Granada was amazing and I was working for Carolyn Reynolds who was executive producer of *Coronation Street*. I was working for her on things like *Families*, *Revelations* and *Children's Ward*.

NG: *So* Coronation Street *was a good experience?*

SW: I had a fantastic time when I got on to *Coronation Street*. You were working with brilliant writers like Peter Whalley and Stephen Mallatratt. Amazing names I'd seen on screen since I was 13 and then you're in the room with them once a fortnight. I never spoke for the first three years because I was in awe of everyone. Just being in that environment where you were learning how to tell cracking stories was extraordinary. On *Coronation Street* the writers were the most important element of the whole thing. I think even on a par with the actors; the writers were really, really respected. When I worked on *Emmerdale* script editors rewrote your scripts and that was partly why I left. I wasn't having that; I wasn't having my name on something that someone else had written. You come to *Coronation Street* and they don't touch your script. You got notes and you did them yourself and you knew that what went out on screen was your work. There is a real pride in that and I've always been very insistent that the script should be respected. You've got your name on it and, if there's something in there you're not happy with, you don't let it go out with your name on.

NG: *So you reach* Coronation Street. *Did you know where you wanted to go then?*

SW: Yes, I did because I worked with Kay Mellor a lot. Kay had very briefly written on *Corrie*, but by that stage she had done *Band of Gold* and she'd got a new series *Playing the Field*. She invited me on board for the second series and it was the first time I'd been asked to write a nine o'clock hour-long BBC1 drama. Kay was my role model at the time. I had always aspired to write *Coronation Street* and I thought I'd be on there for ever, up until meeting Kay. When Kay was doing big nine o'clock dramas I thought: 'That's what *I* want to do next. If Kay can do it, I can do it.' She was really supportive. So my ambition was to get my own drama. I did have the experience of writing for Tiger Aspect on *Playing the Field*, which was a whole different ball game; so much bigger, more demanding, so many more notes about getting it exactly right and the timescale was different. I was just seduced by the better production values they have on bigger dramas.

NG: *Were you working on* At Home with the Braithwaites *then?*

SW: When I was writing *Corrie* I talked to Tony Wood about writing a sitcom about a family. Tony originally commissioned *Braithwaites* as a half-hour sitcom about this dysfunctional family. They hadn't won the lottery. They were just a bunch of people who didn't get on with each other. You couldn't quite work out why they were all in the same house, other than they were related to each other. I wrote it as a sitcom and then Tony left and Carolyn inherited it and she commissioned it as an hour-long drama.

NG: *Did she call you in and say 'I've seen this but I think it would make an hour-long drama'?*

SW: By that stage, anyway, I'd been doing other stuff. She'd had an idea for a drama about mountain rescue for ITV. She'd ask me on board to do it. She obviously had a lot of faith in me and she knew I had experience on *Playing the Field*. She obviously thought I was becoming that calibre of writer. So when she inherited the *Braithwaites* project she said, 'Why don't we do this at nine o'clock but make it more serious.' I don't think comedy-drama had been invented! *Braithwaites* and *Cold Feet* kind of defined what we now think of as comedy-drama. So I rewrote...

NG: *When did the idea of the lottery win come into it?*

SW: I can't remember at what point this woman winning all this money became a factor. Originally, it wasn't to do with the lottery; it was to do with her getting a telephone bill where they accidently credited her account with a ridiculous amount of money. It was meant to be the joke of trying to ring British Telecom but never getting through to the right person. Eventually, she gives up and thinks, 'I'll keep the money.' Then the lottery thing happened. ITV did this big lottery-related evening. I think it was the first night of *Who Wants to be a Millionaire?* so we had a fantastic inheritance. The audience went from *Who Wants to be a Millionaire?* straight into *At Home with the Braithwaites*. We got 9 million on that first episode.

NG: *It must have seemed so easy?*

SW: It wasn't plain sailing. We sent it to Nick Elliott, who was in charge of ITV then, and we got all these notes back saying 'I don't get that', 'I don't know what it is' and we thought it was dead in the water. Apparently, David Liddiment leaned on Nick and said, 'Just greenlight it,' and he did. Nick was really proud of it when it came out. The thing is drama is subject to people's whims and tastes and you're never quite sure where you stand.

NG: *Did you work to an end point? Did you know how it was going to end?*

SW: You work from series to series; you never know whether you are going to get another series. It's like *Scott & Bailey* – I'm so glad we got a second series but we don't know whether we'll get a third. We are optimistic that we will, but you never really know. Apart from that *Scott & Bailey*, *Braithwaites* is the only time I've had a second series in ten years. No matter how successful you think you are, it is never easy.

NG: *Did you feel any pressure or were you just delighted to get it?*

SW: I was absolutely delighted. It does do your head in sometimes and having to write two episodes of the *Braithwaites* in one week at one point, which basically meant being locked in Carolyn's office and not being able to sleep but you kind of love it at the same time. It's mad!

I think how lucky am I doing a job I've always wanted to do. I have a different agent now – I'm with Bethan Evans now – she's very good at getting things through. I've always had a lot of control over what I do. I think I've had a lot of control since the *Braithwaites* as I got really angry that a lot decisions were made without me. People sort of deciding that it was their show rather than mine. Initially, I was associate producer. In a way it is just a title but it means you are more involved and people have to invite you to meetings. Now I'm co-executive producer with Nicola Shindler on *Scott & Bailey*, although Nicola is the one who carries all the responsibility. You're a bit invisible as the writer because nobody sees you work. Everyone sees the crew and actors working. No one sees what you do. You're sort of someone who disappears after production begins.

NG: *Do you get more noes than yeses?*

SW: I usually get things commissioned to script but that's when, particularly at the BBC, you fall down. I wrote a project for the BBC about three years ago now and it went into that stupid situation you only get with the BBC – ITV don't do it – ITV will say yes or no. BBC don't actually say no and they don't say yes and so you end up with: 'Can you write it as a two-parter?' That doesn't work: 'Can you write it as a 90-minuter?' 'No, we actually like it as a two-parter.' You just want to know and you end up fighting about it. They don't know what they want. That's why I like working with Nicola because she knows what she wants and you achieve very tangible results. Whereas at the BBC you just feel you are in a very vague place; people don't know quite what they want.

NG: *With* The Amazing Mrs Pritchard, *did you know that story was going to be told over six episodes or did you expect that to come back?*

SW: I wanted it to come back. I'd hoped it would come back. I didn't know what was going to happen in the whole six episodes when it was greenlit. I'd gone in with this brilliant idea of a cabinet of women. I think that was the hardest thing I'd ever written. I had a political advisor who was brilliant but the amount of research I had to do was the equivalent of doing a degree in politics in about six weeks. It was quite scary because I didn't know after Episode 1 what was going to happen.

That's often the way, you know. We got Series 2 of *Scott & Bailey* and we had a lot of ideas but we didn't know where it was heading. I'm writing Episode 8 now. I've kind of just decided what happens in Episode 8 because of the speed you have to turn these things around. They commissioned it three months later this year than they commissioned it last year. ITV wanted to transmit it earlier than they did last year and they also wanted two more episodes. Essentially, we have got a lot less time to make more episodes. You try to make it as considered and thoughtful as you can, but essentially you are making it up as you go along. It is having the confidence to do that. It's having the confidence to take your time when you know you haven't got time!

NG: *How do you find handing your characters over to another writer?*

SW: It's hard. It's one of the hardest things in the world because it's evolving as you're doing it. A writer came in, and it's not her fault, but it just didn't work. It wasn't what she did was bad; it just wasn't part of the evolving thing.

NG: *In that instance, were they pitching an episode or were you giving them the episode?*

SW: We went in giving her ideas about what she should do but a lot of stuff was the continuity with the personal side. I modelled *Scott & Bailey* on *Nurse Jackie* because I love *Nurse Jackie*, in that every episode is a complex weave of about 300 stories! And when you tell stories very lightly, you can tell one story in three scenes. As my script editor says: 'You don't need to see people buying the milk to make the tea; you want to see them drink the tea.' It's that kind of show where you really attack your stories, and to do that with the continuity of the characters is really tough. The only script that has worked out is written by Amelia Bullmore who plays DCI Gill Murray and that's because she knows the characters as well as I do. She has that minute knowledge of those things. It is really hard for other people coming in to do it. I've been there when I did *Playing the Field*.

NG: *Did you find the urge to want to change things or did you leave it to the script editors to sort?*

SW: It is really interesting because when I saw the script I thought – and she is a really good writer – I just wanted to get hold of it and change it, whereas the one Amelia has written, I absolutely don't want to touch it. She's got the voices right, she's got the humour. It is a really tough call.

NG: *How did you approach developing your own material like* Scott & Bailey? *Do you come up with a concept? I know there was an idea that Suranne and Sally Lindsay had and then there was this other idea through Diane Taylor?*

SW: Sally and Suranne came up with the idea of being *Cagney & Lacey* in Manchester. They wrote a document with various stories about female working detectives, but it was about them being in Division. I wrote the original script with them being in Division, which is general crime. That got turned down by ITV and the BBC. We were filming *Unforgiven* and the production designer on that, Grant Montgomery, and I were chatting. He'd worked on *See No Evil.* I was interested in Myra Hindley at the time. He said you've got to meet Diane Taylor. He said you'll get on with her like a house on fire. We met and we did and we really got on straight away. She had worked all her life in homicide. What happened was ITV just changed their mind and said they did want *Scott & Bailey.* I think this was after *Unforgiven* had been on and that worked really well. I think they wanted me to write something else with Suranne in. So they decided to go with *Scott & Bailey*, but because I'd met Di by then I decided to change it completely. It became about them being in the Major Incident Team. The whole thing was going to be about murder. It just became more vibrant, more dark.

NG: *Character or concept first? With* Unforgiven *I assume the central character was your starting point?*

SW: I think the concept and the main character are closely knitted together. You start with a germ of an idea and then the rest is hard work. With *Unforgiven* I decided to do a story about this woman who was in prison and what it must be like to come out after 15 years. The rest of the story was just hard work after having that initial kernel of an idea.

NG: *Knowing what Ruth in* Unforgiven *was supposed to have done and you don't really know until right at the end. Obviously you, as the writer, know, but the audience doesn't. To all intents and purposes this is an unpleasant character. How do you take the audience with you?*

SW: I didn't know actually because the way it transpires in the original idea for the story she really did kill the policeman. It was only when I got on to write the final episode and I had a conversation with Nicola from which came the idea of 'What if she didn't do it?' That was unique. In my mind, Ruth was always heroic no matter if she had done it. Somebody who was born in a very difficult situation, and did the best she could, found herself on the wrong side of the law, in a situation but for the grace of God any of us could have chosen to do the wrong thing in the heat of the moment. I found her quite heroic. For me it was the fact that she was clearly broken when she comes out and has no confidence. She's still sort of slightly aggressive but you can see she has been absolutely destroyed by what she has been through. I think there is a massive amount of sympathy for her when you first see her, even though she is a tough-looking woman. And by making little elements like when she carries that bloke's shopping upstairs – I mean, she doesn't have to. You think she's going to nick it but she doesn't. It is little things like that where you can see in that character in any other circumstances she has a heart of gold. Born in any other world she would be a really perfectly nice person.

NG: *What advice would you give to new writers? In the end all those writers need to be better than you or at least on a par?*

SW: I think you've just got be passionate about it. I think you know if you are. I was obsessed with writing from about 13. I use to spend a lot of time being shut in my room being sad, writing. I don't think I was sad because I loved it. Right from an early age you just know you're going to get there because it's your passion. The only advice I can give is be honest about how passionate you are. Even if you're like me, I was just so shy but I was never shy about trying to put my work out there and trying to do things with it. I found it hard but I did it because I knew I had to do it because I was absolutely driven to it. There was no way I *wasn't* going to do it. I think you have to have the courage of your passion and obsessiveness.

15

....

Where to send your script

In this chapter you will learn:
- *about the BBC's Writersroom*
- *about various initiatives and competitions in the UK and US that offer new or relatively new writers routes into the industry*
- *how to get – and keep – an agent.*

_____

BBC Writersroom

> *'Our job is to take scripts as a means to an end and that end is people rather than things. So scripts are things that lead us to people and if the scripts are good we assume the people are interesting. We'll lead them to other people in the BBC and that's when you start talking about things.'*

> Paul Ashton, BBC Writersoom

The BBC Writersroom is a unique institution. It accepts unsolicited scripts – around 10,000 every year – and its primary remit is to uncover new UK-based writers, champion them and try to help them into the industry.

Once you've completed your script and made it the best you can, you will need to download a cover sheet from the Writersroom website to send with your script and include an stamped addressed envelope if you want the script returned.

The BBC Writersroom has three windows a year in which writers can send scripts to the Script Room – Spring, Autumn and New Year. All the scripts received during each window are dealt with as one group. The process is as follows:

1 Initially, the first ten pages of the script are read. Based on those opening ten pages the script reader will either decide to read on or pass and return it to the writer. The latter is the fate for around 80 per cent of the scripts submitted.
2 The next stage is a full script read. Once again, some of those scripts will now be returned to writers, who will get a brief script report and feedback.
3 The remainder that have impressed will be put forward for the Script Room. This group of writers will have direct contact with the Writersroom team and be offered master classes and/or workshops. These have the goal of helping the writer to make useful contacts with people in the industry, which could potentially lead to representation by an agent or a commission.

In addition, the BBC Writersroom also runs one-off competitions and specific initiatives with other industry partners.

There is a wealth of free information on the BBC Writersroom website including blogs, articles, tips, advice and a library of downloadable BBC TV, film and radio scripts. In terms of television drama, there are episodes from series, serials, one-offs and continuing drama.

Details: www.bbc.co.uk/writersroom

Competitions and other scriptwriting initiatives

Scriptwriting competitions and initiatives have become a way of unearthing new talent for both agents and producers and really do open doors for some scriptwriters. However, there is a plethora of different competitions and not all are beneficial to the writer. Before entering, you need to check the credentials of the competition. Ask these questions:

▶ Who is running it?
▶ Who is judging it?

- ▶ What are the benefits for the winning writers?
- ▶ Exactly who are the industry contacts which the competition promises to pass the best scripts on to?
- ▶ What are the success stories?

Also be wary of 'terms and conditions' since some unscrupulous competitions get you to sign over the rights to your scripts. The established, good ones don't.

The best competitions have a lot of credibility in the industry and, if you achieve something with these competitions, it is worth adding this to your CV. Also, note that some competitions have an entry fee. This is not necessarily a negative thing but only you can judge whether a particular competition is worth the investment of your hard-earned money. As I've said before, however, if *you* are not willing to invest in yourself then why should others?

Below are some of the leading competitions and initiatives in the UK and US.

BBC WRITERS' ACADEMY

'You can't teach writing. What you can teach is structure, and if writers master that, it allows them access to their voice – and it is those voices that will keep the industry thriving.'

John Yorke, Controller of Drama Production

The BBC Writers' Academy was conceived by the BBC's Controller of Drama Production, John Yorke. Each year the academy selects eight writers to undergo an intensive 15-month training programme designed to equip them with all the skills necessary to write successfully for BBC Drama. The selected writers write a broadcast episode of *Doctors* and, if successful, will write commissioned episodes for *Casualty*, *Holby City* and *EastEnders*.

Eligible are writers who have had, and can prove they have had, at least one paid commission for radio, theatre, film or television. Academy writers have included Mark Catley, Daisy Coulam, Rachel Flowerday, Ian Kershaw, Karen Laws and Justin Young.

Details: www.bbc.co.uk/writersroom/about/the-writers-academy

COMING UP

'There is a lot of really interesting new talent out there. We've seen that from the results we've had over the years on Coming Up. For us it's an opportunity to find, work with and nurture some pretty exciting new talent. The likes of Jack Thorne, Jann Demange, Tom Harper – all sorts of interesting writers and directors have come through Coming Up who then go on and work for all sorts of people, but they've often gone to work for Channel 4 as well.'

Ben Stoll, Channel 4 Development Executive

Coming Up is currently the only talent scheme in the UK where emerging film-makers have the opportunity to make an authored drama with a guaranteed network broadcast. Launched in 2002 by Channel 4 and Touchpaper Television, the aim of the scheme is to create eye-catching, innovative, challenging films.

For successful applicants, the scheme can lead to an original 30-minute film on Channel 4. Coming Up looks for scripts which are bold and original and which feature surprising ideas, and for strong voices that are unafraid of ambition, wit, urgency and fearless entertainment. The budgets are limited, so the scripts must be able to be shot in four days.

To apply, writers must not have had an original single, series or serial broadcast on UK television. Writers who have contributed episodes to series and serials (e.g. a long-running soap) are now also eligible to apply. The scheme is also open to directors without a primetime TV drama credit.

Details: www.touchpapertv.com

4 SCREENWRITING

'The intention is to give writers from all sorts of different backgrounds and disciplines the opportunity to experience the development process. The idea is over the course of how many months those writers will attend various workshops, meetings and will work with a script editor on a new script. Nearly all of these writers haven't been through that development process. It's a very valuable learning scheme.'

Ben Stoll, Channel 4 Development Executive

The 4 Screenwriting Competition is an annual event run by Channel 4 and was launched in 2010. It is open only to writers who do not have a broadcast credit as a television or film writer (although short films of 20 minutes or less are exempt).

The competition is launched in the autumn when writers need to submit an original writing sample of a minimum of 30 minutes along with their CV. In 2011/12 there were approximately 3,000 entries.

Twelve people are selected for a place on a course which gives an insight into how TV drama, with a Channel 4 slant, works. Over a five-month period each writer gets to work on their own one-hour pilot script for an original series or serial, alongside an experienced script editor. In addition, they attend two weekends of talks and script meetings at Channel 4. A small fee is paid for attending the course.

Many writers who have taken part in the scheme have got noticed. Channel 4 commissioned a different version of one of the projects developed on the course; a second writer has been commissioned via an independent project, while two others have gone on to earn broadcast credits on Coming Up.

Details: www.4talent.Channel4.com or www.script-consultant.co.uk

RED PLANET PRIZE

> '*Drama in this country is written by the same 12 old farts – and I include myself in that – you've got to have new blood coming through. You need the next generation of writers, so that was the idea of the prize really. The Red Planet Prize is to find the next generation of writers.*'

Tony Jordan, Scriptwriter and Executive Producer, Red Planet Pictures

The Red Planet Prize was launched by Tony Jordan in 2007 in order to nurture aspiring writers and find new talent through his production company, Red Planet Pictures. The annual competition, run in partnership with Kudos Film and Television, awards the winner £5,000 and entry into a mentoring scheme. Other writers who impress may also find their way onto the mentoring scheme.

The RPP's biggest success has been the finalist Robert Thorogood who created and wrote an eight-part detective series, *Death in Paradise,* that was a hit on BBC1 in 2011 and was immediately recommissioned for a second series. Two other writers, Chris Lindsay and Malcolm McGonigle, joined the writing team on *MI High*, a Kudos production for CBBC.

To enter, writers are invited, once the competition opens, to submit the first ten pages of their script of a 60-minute episode of their original television series. Those who impress in those opening ten pages are invited to submit the full script for the second round. It is from those full script reads that the eventual winner is chosen, along with other selected writers invited to participate in the mentoring scheme. In 2011/12 there were more than 2,000 entries.

Details: www.redplanetpictures.co.uk/prize

BBC WRITERSROOM

'We do more competitions and talent searches now and more one-off things, which means I think you get a slightly better balance between the rolling scripts and putting up a brief to write a studio sitcom to be judged by Dawn French. That's a great thing to go for, and people go 'OK, I could have my script read by the judges' – one of those judges is Dawn French and one of those judges is Controller of Comedy Commissioning. What chances are you going to get unless you've got a really great agent? What a position to be in.'

Paul Ashton, BBC Writersroom

The BBC Writersroom does run script competitions from time to time and it is worth looking on its pages. Indeed, the BBC Writersroom's 'Opportunities' page lists leading competitions and initiatives, covering not just television but also radio and theatre.

The competitions are usually run with partners who have a specific goal in mind. CBBC, for example, looks for writers who want to write for children. Some competitions may have a geographical restriction with the aim of uncovering local talent in certain areas.

BAFTA ROCLIFFE FORUM

The BAFTA Rocliffe Forum is a fantastic initiative that exposes the writer's work to the industry and can lead to the writer attracting the attention of agents, producers and commissioners.

The competition invites you to submit a 10 to 12-page section, with accompanying context documents, of your script with the potential to be performed on stage. There is a small entry fee. The judges, all of whom work within the industry, whittle down the scripts to a maximum long list of 25. From the long list, three are selected to have their 10–12 page performed on stage with professional actors, receive feedback from a leading industry professional (Julian Fellowes, Peter Kosminsky and Christine Langan have been previous participants) before an audience featuring representatives from agencies and production companies.

Details: www.rocliffe.com or www.bafta.org

SCRIPTAPALOOZA TV WRITING COMPETITION

> 'The goal of Scriptapalooza TV is to connect writers with producers, managers, and agents ... people that can make a difference in a writer's career.

Scriptapalooza website

The Scriptapalooza TV Writing Competition is a well-respected annual event in the US and was first launched in 2002. The top cash prize is low (only $500 in 2012), but the 12 winners – that is, the top three in the respective pilot, half-hour, one hour and reality show categories – are promoted within the industry.

In terms of drama, the competition has a category for pilots, namely, original scripts. The other category is the one-hour programme which accepts spec scripts of existing US TV shows. So if you have the urge to write for your favourite show and play with your favourite characters, then this is the category for you.

There is an entry fee with a discount if you submit early.

Some of the winners each year have managed to gain representation as a result of their success in the competition.

Details: www.scriptapaloozatv.com

SCRIPT PIPELINE TV WRITING COMPETITION

The Script Pipeline TV Writing Competition is another US competition launched in 2007/08. In terms of television drama, the competition has categories of original pilot and a spec script of an existing show. It has a top cash prize of $1,500 (2012) and the winners' details and their work are put before the industry. Again, being placed in this competition has helped some writers get meetings and has led to representation.

Details: www.scriptpipeline.com/tv-writing-competition

WRITERS ON THE VERGE

Writers on the Verge is an NBC-backed initiative to uncover new talent and is not open to any writer with staff experience. To apply, applicants must write and submit a script based on a show that aired new episodes in the current season prior to the application period. They also need to fill out an application form, submit their CV/résumé and sign a release form for their submitted script.

The successful applicants gain a place on the 12-week Writers on the Verge course in Los Angeles. The course consists of two night classes, the focus of which is to create an exceptional spec script. The course does not include accommodation and transport.

Participants have gone on to write for shows such as *Burn Notice*, *Chuck*, *Friday Night Lights* and *White Collar*.

Details: www.nbcunicareers.com/earlyprograms/writersontheverge

WARNER BROS. TV WRITERS' WORKSHOP

For over 30 years, the Warner Bros. Television Writers' Workshop has been the premier US writing programme for new writers looking to start and further their career in the world of television. The list of graduates who have gone on to do great things is long, including Terrance Winter (*Boardwalk Empire*) and Marc Cherry (*Desperate Housewives*).

Every year, the workshop selects up to ten participants out of almost 2,000 submissions and exposes them to Warner Bros. Television's top writers and executives, all with the ultimate goal of earning them a staff position on a Warner Bros.-produced television show.

Applications must be made during a one-month window in May of each year when writers are invited to submit a writing sample of a primetime or cable network show that aired new episodes during the previous television season.

Details: www.writersworkshop.warnerbros.com

FOX WRITERS INTENSIVE

The Fox Writers Intensive (FWI) is a highly selective writers' initiative, held at the Fox Studios in Los Angeles. The intensive course is designed to introduce experienced writers with unique voices, backgrounds, and life and professional experiences that reflect the diverse perspectives of US audiences to a wide range of Fox staff writers, showrunners, directors, screenwriters and creative executives. The scheme works with the selected writers to build on both their general craft and the business of writing for television, feature films and digital content with the added goal of creating a viable source of experienced staff.

FWI is for trained writers and/or previously staffed writers who have a strong command of their craft and who are deeply committed to pursuing that craft as their profession. A maximum of ten candidates are invited to participate.

Details: www.fox.com/fwi

Agents and literary managers

To get an agent, the first thing you have to do is write a script, preferably two, and be working on a third and have loads of ideas. These scripts need to be good and they will need to stand out. The agent will have to feel passionate about the script if they are going to promote it (and you), either as a spec to get you an assignment or to try and sell it with the goal of getting it commissioned.

Remember you are competing against thousands of other writers all of whom are also seeking representation. So the quality of the script and the originality of your voice are very important. It should not be derivative or obviously sound like anyone else.

There are a finite number of agents and a finite number of clients any one agent can manage. If they are going to take you on, it may involve another writer being released. For them to do that, they want to be sure that their investment in you is going to pay off and that is why they want to know if you are more than a 'one script wonder'.

You will need to impress them and show you have a commitment to writing. Agents will want to know what other endeavours you have made. Have you done any other writing, for example? Have you written for the theatre or for radio? Have you made any short films? Are you involved in the industry in some other capacity? Have you entered and had any success in any reputable writing competitions? Have you undertaken any reputable writing courses? Have you formed any relationships with or gained referrals from anyone within the industry? What industry events have you attended?

Increasingly, it is getting harder to get people to read your work and, when someone says they will, it can take a very long time for them to do so and get back to you.

HOW TO CONTACT AN AGENT

▶ Write your script.
▶ Research the agents available. Look at publications such as the *Writers' & Artists' Yearbook* (in the UK) and *Writer's Market* (in the US) and look online at agents' websites. Also, if you are able, research individual agents. Read or view or listen to any interviews they have given and look at their client list.
▶ Check whether their preferred method of approach is it by email or letter or by referral.
▶ Write a brief but polite email/letter introducing yourself and attached your writing CV/résumé. You can add the title and logline of the script you wish them to read.
▶ Do not send a script unless it is asked for.
▶ If an agent does invite you to send them a sample of your work, establish whether they want an electronic or paper copy. Make it a pristine copy. You should also ask if they want scene numbering or not, in case they wish to make any specific comments about the script.
▶ Be patient. Agents are busy people and so you may have to wait a while before they read and respond to your script. They may say at the outset how long it could take – you may have to wait several months. Follow up ten weeks after submitting and politely enquire about your script's status.

THE REPLY

There are two broad categories (of course):

Reply 1 The agent, after reading your script, says no. They may state a reason why or they may not. Thank them politely for taking the time for reading. You may either need to relook at the script or it may be a matter of taste. A rejection doesn't stop you approaching another agent.

Reply 2   Your writing piques their interest and the agent invites you for a meeting.

THE MEETING AND AFTER

As with every meeting or interview, prepare well and be yourself. Do not make claims you cannot substantiate. Agents are savvy people; they will know.

During or after the meeting they may invite you to submit something else. They may keep the door open and, if you're lucky, agree to represent you.

If you do get representation with an agent, it does not mean you have made it. You still have to write. An agent cannot help you to write. They can be an independent set of eyes when reading your work and their knowledge can potentially direct your work to the right producer, indie or broadcaster. On the strength of your writing – by which I mean your completed scripts – they can get you meetings that can lead to assignments on continuing drama or other shows, or even your own series, but all that depends on you continuing to write.

Being a television drama scriptwriter is largely about series writing. Series writing – that is, writing to somebody else's format – is most writers' bread and butter. Agents have to be able to believe you will be able to do that, so that both you and they can earn some sort of living.

And remember: there will be somebody like you looking for representation and approaching your agent. If they are impressed with that newcomer, they may have to cull someone from their client list – you don't want it to be you.

New writers can sometimes focus too much on trying to secure an agent. In some ways it can lead them into believing it is the ultimate goal, that you *must* have an agent to get into the industry. There are myriad different ways to enter into the industry and, once you have and you do get a commission, you will certainly require an agent. Agents will be definitely more interested if you have carved out your own road and have the writing and talent to support it.

> **Key advice**
>
> ▶ In the UK the BBC's Writersroom offers a unique opportunity for new scriptwriters – try it.
> ▶ Competitions provide another valuable route into the industry as well as providing you with a goal (and a deadline).
> ▶ You don't have to have an agent, but they do have the experience of the industry that you don't yet have and can gain you opportunities that you would not otherwise be able to access.
> ▶ Agents are busy people – be patient with them.

Industry interview 7: the executive producer

Francis Hopkinson is the Creative Director of Drama for ITV Studios. ITV Studios is seen as an independent production company but it primarily supplies programming to the UK broadcaster ITV. Hopkinson has worked for Granada, Channel 4 and Left Bank Pictures and his producing credits include Always and Everyone, The Jury, Colditz, Henry VIII, Murder City *and, as an executive producer,* Wallander, Married Single Other *and* DCI Banks.

Nicholas Gibbs: *What did you learn script editing for* The Bill?

Francis Hopkinson: *The Bill* was quite unique as a long-running serial. Every story was individual, so every writer had their own story but they just had to use the regular repertory of actors. It was much more like development. *The Bill* was unique in that way. It was a great place to learn. One week you could have one story that was a car chase; the next week it could be two people sitting in a room; it could be a murder investigation or a slice of life.

NG: *That was the half-hour* Bill?

FH: Yes, 1995. We were doing 150 episodes a year so you learned incredibly quickly. They were short stories before it became a soap. A writer would come in, pitch an idea, you would work on the idea and that would go before a committee of producers, then it became storylined, then a script. In a couple of months you could see your stuff on screen. As a script editor, you could see what worked and what didn't work. It also meant you were working with writers as, I think, a script editor should work, with a writer as a kind of advisor, good friend, an encourager, advocate and cajoler. It was really good and stood everyone in good stead. Of all the team we had on *The Bill*, all have gone on to greater things within the industry. It was such a great learning ground for script editors. Most of them have gone on to producing. A couple of them are now running their own independent production companies. One of them has just become a writer and got a book deal. It was a great place to learn and you learn very quickly.

NG: *When did you go into producing?*

FH: Tony Garnett wanted to do a police series and he asked me what I would do. I said I'd break all the rules that were on *The Bill*. He said that's what he wanted to do. Tony gave me the licence to do that using some of the writers from *The Bill*. We did a lot of research and created a series called *Cops*. Series 1 won a BAFTA as did the second series. I wasn't working as a producer; I was called an Associate Producer. The producer was a guy called Eric Coulter and I watched what he was doing and realized I could do it. I thought I could see what producing is and I might be able to do some of it, if not all of it. Eric was a very good adviser and Granada, as it then was, offered me a chance to create and produce a medical series which was called *Always and Everyone*. And that's kind of how I moved into producing. I worked on that for a couple of years and worked in another department with Andy Harries at Granada for five years. I went to Channel 4 as a commissioning editor for a couple years, then started an independent with Andy Harries because I enjoyed working with him. After five years I was asked to come back to ITV.

NG: *So is ITV Studios seen as an independent?*

FH: Yes. When I worked for ITV seven years ago they had five drama departments. They had the Drama Department run by Andy Harries; one run by Michelle Buck; they had two in Manchester effectively; and Keith Richardson, who ran Yorkshire TV. However, due to changes in the industry, all those drama departments but one disappeared. So I've been asked to come in to help build the drama capacity. ITV as a company wants to have the majority of its programmes made by its own independent production company, ITV Studios.

NG: *How does the process work with you? How do people approach you?*

FH: We are normally approached by agents or we approach agents. We have an idea for which we look for a writer, or a writer approaches us with an idea through their agent and then we discuss it. We normally go to treatment. We go to treatment without discussing it with people, but before we go to script we would normally discuss it with a broadcaster to try and get a sense if they want it.

NG: *You don't automatically think, 'This is for ITV' – you look to find a broadcaster for the project?*

FH: I'm looking for ITV projects. That's my brief. That's the market that is closest to us and most open to us. We will talk to everyone who will have our ideas but primarily we will talk to ITV. In a way, it's not a formal first-look deal but everything we do will probably be seen by ITV before it goes anywhere else.

NG: *When you approach ITV commissioning do you go in with a treatment at that stage?*

FH: We normally talk with a verbal pitch first and if they like it a) to make sure they haven't got anything similar, which is broadly when an idea can fall, and b) you have to see if they like it and quite often they will like it. We've all got a pretty good idea what ITV want, so very rarely do they say that's not going to be right for ITV. More often they have an idea that's similar. Normally, we have regular meetings where we will pitch stuff verbally. If they like it, we'll go to treatment or we'll send them the treatment we've got and then take it from there.

NG: *Is there a possibility for unsolicited scripts to be taken up? BBC has the Writersroom but ITV doesn't have an equivalent really, does it?*

FH: In a way, the agents are the first point of entry for us. It's not that we don't feel we have an obligation to the undiscovered talent out there. It is really just because we couldn't cope if we had a load of scripts pouring in. The BBC does have a structure to deal with that.

NG: *Agents can act as quality filters for you in the first instance?*

FH: The agent's raw material is writers, so in a way that's the way they've got to go. Agents will filter them. Some of the agents will help train them in many ways but the agents are the first way in.

NG: *Do you have a preferred set of agents whose judgement you trust more than others?*

FH: There are certain agents I trust more than others. With the top agencies, when you get a script from them you'll think you'll drop everything to read it or just think it's going to be better.

NG: *Agents have suggested that the BBC and ITV want A-list writers?*

FH: The problem with A-list writers is that they are very busy. Some of them are arguably taking on too much and probably need a break. I certainly think, and I'm sure the BBC feels this, that the pool needs to be widened. We got to the situation two or three years ago where Channel 4, ITV and BBC were all chasing the same writers, but I think some of the work wasn't that great. I think everyone accepts and knows that we've got to find more writers. There are certain writers who become A-list; certain writers who do quite a lot of work on series and then they do something outstanding and they become A-list. I think it would be very destructive if there was just a set list of people we only worked from. We've got to widen that pool.

NG: *What judgements do you make on whose projects you choose to pursue? What are the criteria once you've got those ideas in front of you?*

FH: You're just looking for an interesting idea. It's the idea that appeals to you. That literally is all it is. You have to ask yourself the question: Can the writer deliver? Which is why a lot of people turn to the A-list because they have done it before, but more and more you talk to the writer about the idea and see what they want to do with it. You get a sense of their ambition. Essentially, you're looking at the idea that could be interesting. The first question is: Would I want to see this? And then you think: Can I sell it?

NG: *You've got to pick things that people want to watch for ITV?*

FH: One of things I've always liked about working for ITV is that it is quite straightforward. If people don't watch your show, you have failed. What critics say doesn't really matter. What people are tweeting or blogging doesn't really matter. People have to watch your show. The difference between a hit and miss is very clear.

NG: *What is the process once you've commissioned someone, say, for a six-part series?*

FH: Each time differs. Normally, if you were commissioning a six-parter, you would normally get the lead writer to write as much of that series as you could. Six hours might have six months before you go into pre-production. That is quite a lot for a lead writer so you probably give the lead writer half or four of those. It's a sort of impossible question to answer.

NG: *Do you look to try and get all the scripts ready before you go into production?*

FH: That's a luxury and it would be great if you could do that. I have done that and I have to say it has always worked very well, but it doesn't happen very often. If the team gets the commission for a three-parter, you'd have all three scripts but for a six-parter you rarely do. On *Cops*, which was eight parts, we had all the scripts before we started and it made a huge difference. It's great if that happens, but it happens very rarely when you get a commission; it is usually after two scripts. So that's when you try and catch up with yourself.

NG: *Is that down to late commissioning decisions?*

FH: I think it is but I also think there are a lot of companies whose livelihoods are dependent on knowing quickly. They can't sit around and get more scripts commissioned. They need to get things into production. I think it is possibly late decisions. It is also very difficult to motivate writers if they don't think it is going to get made. Often you need the finishing line in front of you to get everyone to go. So it would be great to have more time, but at the same time it is not good to have more time. Deadlines are good.

NG: *Do you do co-productions with smaller companies if they come to you with an idea?*

FH: We can do. With the margins of drama so small, it has to be a pretty sensational idea to do it or with big talent, big off-screen or on-screen talent, to make it worth our while.

NG: *Do you look at casting at early stage? If someone says this is the part for so-and-so, do you look on it more favourably? Certainly, a few years ago there were handcuff deals with certain actors.*

FH: You do look at casting. It helps. I try to have a cast in my mind when I send in a script to ITV because I think it helps visualize it. It's always useful to say to writers: Who do you have in mind for that?

NG: *Are you looking for a named star that the audience will recognize for those key roles? Very few ITV things come in with actors that are not known.*

FH: It certainly helps but there aren't that many of those people. A bit like the writers, the audience will quickly become tired of someone who would guarantee you a commission. I think there are very few actors who are absolutely guaranteed to get you a certain amount of viewers. Good casting is more important: a good actor in a surprising role or a surprising actor in a good role. It worked for us with Ken Branagh in *Wallander*. He hadn't been on television for quite some time. It was a surprising thing for him to do. He loved the books so he wanted to do it. I think the audience were very intrigued by that. It could have had a more familiar face but I don't think they would have been as intrigued by it.

NG: *ITV have 13 cop series either in development, on screen or about to hit the screens, but they say they are trying to get away from being seen as the crime channel. Does that colour the way you look at the projects that come into you?*

FH: I think the bedrock of ITV, of all television, is crime drama. Everyone goes on about American television but it is actually mostly procedural crime. Everyone keeps going on about *Mad Men* but that is one series in among 50. I do think you can make more of an impact if you find something fresh. It could be a crime drama like *Sherlock* or a costume drama like *Downton Abbey*. I think television channels have to be a fairly rich banquet. The argument for doing drama on Channel 4 was that the schedule looked a bit more exciting. If you just do crime drama, it gets harder and harder. There is the law of diminishing returns. There always comes a point when people go: 'I don't want to see another crime drama.' But we are looking at crime dramas but we are thinking about how to make them different and we're definitely looking at other things.

NG: *Do you find you get derivative crime dramas in the wake of* The Killing *or costume dramas that try to mimic* Downton Abbey *sent to you?*

FH: No. There's only room for a couple of shows like *Downton* on the channel and the truth is that, while there were a lot of people who talked about watching *The Killing*, it wasn't a big audience or an ITV audience. There are people looking at longer-form crime dramas which are quite interesting. So people talk about a ten-part crime drama rather than a three-part crime drama, which is good. There are certainly lots of shows which are coming out now which are sort of in the *Downton* era. Certainly, I thought people didn't want period drama before *Downton Abbey*. I thought it would be interesting to see if *Downton* worked. It worked so well it told us something about the audience, which is that the audience wanted something different from contemporary drama.

NG: *What was it about* Downton Abbey *that made it such a massive hit?*

FH: *Downton Abbey* does what I think ITV drama does at its best, which is very popular storytelling; it was beautifully made; it felt like a reward when you watched it. Beautifully made, well cast, beautifully acted, great direction. I remember the first episode was brilliantly directed. It took you into that world. It's very well scheduled on a Sunday evening – you really feel it's a treat. ITV drama was always, at its best, very high production values plus a bit of a treat. *Upstairs, Downstairs*, which is obviously an inspiration for *Downton Abbey*, was an ITV show. I think it was in the DNA of ITV. I think that is what you should always be aiming to do.

NG: *What* don't *you like about the approaches made to you or the type of ideas brought to you?*

FH: What I really don't like is television that feels like television. I really don't like something that feels like someone has written television stereotypes. I don't like when it is written by someone who only seems to have watched television rather than getting out. There has to be a knowing a little bit about the world. Where it just feels like a television format, written in television clichés without anything to say about the world, that's what I really don't like.

NG: *Do you gauge that when you meet writers where you've been intrigued by an idea and then learn the writer has been holed up in his room for ten years writing this thing?*

FH: Not at all, because it is about the writer's imagination. I suppose it is about curiosity. I remember a writer – I think it was Tony Marchant but I can never quite remember – and it was a talk and the writer said: 'I write to explore my relationship with the world.' I still think that is the best definition of writing. What you're looking for is a writer's voice even in cop dramas that is exploring the world in some way. I don't want derivative. I don't want cliché. I want something with truth and surprises in it. So when I meet a writer I'm interested in what the writer wants to write about as opposed to what he thinks you want him to write about.

NG: *What don't you like seeing in a script?*

FH: Rarely do I read a script that infuriates me. I have a pet hate which is clichés in a script or something I've seen on television many times before. Sometimes I think the writers have inadvertently plagiarized. I particularly don't like scripts which have a pun on the characters' names. There was one called *Church's Law* and the detective was called Church. That annoys me. I don't know why. Taggart and Inspector Morse are fine but if it was called *Morse Code*... Lack of research is one of the things that really annoy me. When you read a cop script, for example, and it bears no relation to how the police behave. If the writer can't be bothered to research, why on earth should we watch it? When we did *The Cops* the reason it was fresh and good was we spent weeks speaking to the actual police. So we saw a lot of things which we then wrote about through interest in real characters. I remember hearing a writer say he'd done loads of research for another police series which was going out. His research was watching loads of episodes of *Z-Cars*! Again, it's that researching a world as it's seen on television.

NG: *Is it that some writers find research too much effort?*

FH: It is difficult to research the police but you can do it even if it's hanging out by the police station or finding a way in. Ring up and ask; try and find out something. You will normally find someone who is willing to talk. It could be through a friend of a friend who is a policeman. He might give you half an hour. Anything like that. Just do a bit of research. If writers are writing about a newspaper office, go and visit a newspaper office. I remember Stephen Butchard saying to me on the medical series *Always and Everyone* that whenever he'd get stuck he would go down and sit in a hospital and get stories. Don't be shy about doing it. A really well-researched script about a world I don't know will be immediately riveting. Finally, what really annoys me is when they send me a script addressed to Ms Frances Hopkinson! You haven't even bothered to find out who I am.

NG: *What was the big difference between working for a small independent – is there a different outlook as to what you're looking for?*

FH: I find it oddly easier to have the focus of ITV. It really has to be a good idea. The focus of ITV is that we broadly know what we're looking for. What I found hard at an independent was you'd hear an idea and then you would have to think: 'Where can that idea fit?'

NG: *Do you think there is an advantage to writing to ad breaks?*

FH: The ad breaks make a big difference. I do think writers are getting much savvier. The ad break makes a difference how you tell a story, how much story a part has. They do cater for the rhythm of a drama much more. I hadn't made drama for the BBC for a long time and *Wallander* was 89 minutes, but we had to spend a lot of time in the edit suite thinking about the rhythm of the show. Whereas the ad break dictates the rhythm of the show on ITV. I think ITV drama needs a lot more story; you have to drive much more to the ad break to keep people there and indeed make sure people come back the next time. ITV drama is much more specific in its demands.

NG: *How do you handle 'no'?*

FH: I get very frustrated and annoyed when I get a no. When a commissioner says no to you, the commissioners are all very intelligent; they've been hired for their brain and their judgement so you should listen. Normally, after I've gone through the process of being annoyed I accept it. You go back and ask yourself: What didn't work for them in this idea? You work on it again and get a better idea. Actually, when a commissioner says no, it's not because they're wrong, it's because you haven't got it right yet. You've got to accept they didn't quite get it. They haven't quite seen what we're trying to do. Let's see what we've got here and try and make it better.

NG: *What about the reason behind the 'no' when something similar has been on and failed?*

FH: It is quite frustrating when something doesn't work and the commissioner says to you: 'We've just done something about a middle-aged woman. It didn't work so we don't want to do anything about middle-aged women.' You want to say: it didn't work because it wasn't very good. It wasn't the subject matter. So that is kind of frustrating as that does mean that people won't come back to it again. A case in point was a series called *Servants* some years ago which didn't work. So for a long time everyone said no one wants a period series because no one wants to see that sort of thing.

NG: *It's a sort of over-reaction really?*

FH: It became sort of received wisdom and then *Downton Abbey* comes out and shows that it was wrong. It was right for a time. Good stuff is generally watched. My argument is: if it's good and people aren't watching it, then it's not good. Your job is to get people to watch television.

NG: *What advice do you have for writers?*

FH: Write what you want to write, not to please others, because if you write to please yourself at least one person is going to be happy. Write what you want to see. The truth is even the best writers go in and out of fashion but, if they're good, they do come back into fashion. Their skills haven't diminished and they get to write what they want to write.

16

Continuing drama

In this chapter you will learn:
- *about the major continuing dramas in the UK*
- *that each has a unique voice and a unique way of operating*
- *about the intensive scriptwriting process used on these shows.*

Continuing drama, aka soaps, are still by and far away the best route for many writers to get their first writing credit in the UK. These shows are high volume and the most popular on British television. BBC boasts *EastEnders* and daytime drama *Doctors*; ITV has *Coronation Street* and *Emmerdale* in its evening schedules; Channel 4 has the daily teen drama *Hollyoaks*. In addition, the BBC has two primetime year-round weekly medical dramas, *Casualty* and *Holby City*.

In this chapter we look at how these shows work and the opportunities available to writers.

Coronation Street

Coronation Street is ITV's flagship soap drama that screens five times a week and is consistently ITV's most watched drama. Every year the show produces approximately 260 episodes which equates to 130 hours of scripted television drama.

Kieran Roberts *is the executive producer* on Coronation Street *with almost 500 episodes of the show under his belt. He is also ITV's Creative Director of Drama and has overseen such shows as* Cold Blood, Distant Shores, Boy Meets Girl, Blue Murder *and many others.*

Nicholas Gibbs: *What is* Coronation Street?

Kieran Roberts: *Coronation Street* was created in 1960 by an extraordinary man called Tony Warren. In a nutshell it tells the stories, sometimes extraordinary stories, of a group of very ordinary, mostly working-class people living in a cobbled backstreet in a fictional part of Salford. The formula has basically not changed since day one. We tell more stories now and I think it is fair to say our stories are bigger and sometimes more explosive and more action-packed, but the essential formula is being character-driven, female-centric, dramatic but full of warmth and humour.

NG: *How many writers do you have working on* Coronation Street?

KR: It can be between 16 and 20 writers. The way we work it is that all the writing team are all involved in the major decision-making across the entire year. We don't have an inner core of writers who make the decisions and an outer circle of writers who, for example, are just guns for hire. All our writers come to every story conference. So they are allowed to get involved with all our discussions about the stories of all our characters. I think it gives us a sense of continuity and I think it gives them a sense of ownership in all the stories and the characters.

NG: *How do you source new writers for the show?*

KR: Many of the writers on the team have been with us for a long time. We've got one writer who has been with us for 33 years; another writer has been with us 20-odd years; several writers who have been with us between 10 and 15 years. So there is a core of writers who know the show inside out and are absolutely steeped in *Coronation Street.* In terms of new writers, we are very open-minded. Some writers have joined the team with very few credits to their name but with a passion and a real ability. Now if a writer comes to us who is brand new – when I say brand new I don't mean fresh out of college, I mean someone who is still making their mark in the world of professional television scriptwriting – we would as a minimum expect them to write us a trial episode. Quite often we do it twice to be absolutely sure that they can write for this show.

NG: *What are the challenges for a writer joining* Coronation Street?

KR: It's a big machine and they have to operate within it and not outside of it. Some writers, very fine writers, who are used to working on their own or maybe in a partnership with one other writer and creating their own stuff and setting their own deadlines and creating their own working framework, find it very difficult to adapt.

NG: *What is the process from a writing point of view?*

KR: Every three weeks we get together. The producer, assistant producer, story editor, story team, script editors and researcher sit round a table with all the writers. Now it is important that we have all the writers involved in that process all the time and I will say to writers, even if they are taking a bit of time out from writing for us because they are creating a new show, I still want them to come to the story conference. So that's the key moment when we all get together for a day and a half and we make some big decisions, and I want the writer to be part of that process and in fact buy into it. If they have an issue with a character or story, we want to hear it then, not six months later when it's too late.

NG: *What happens at story conference?*

KR: The first morning is the commissioning conference and I'll come back to that because in a sense that is the end of the cycle. In the afternoon we have a story conference which spills into the second day and it goes into the second afternoon until usually four or five o'clock, depending on how well we've done. We talk about stories for the next block of episodes, which is usually three weeks. So that would be typically 15 episodes. We start by saying 'OK, where is everybody now?' And remember where they've come on their journeys. Sometimes we already have a road map for a character or characters and sometimes we have nothing. We literally sit down and say, to give a recent example of stuff that has been on air: 'So, Becky has just found out that Tracy Barlow has lied about pushing her down the stairs causing that miscarriage. What is she going to do? We also know Katherine Kelly, the actress, is leaving and we've got X number of weeks.' So we'll have that discussion. How are we going to map this story out? So we built her this fantastic exit story and we pay off. So we have those discussions about every single character group that's in play. At the end of the conference the writers all go home and they start writing.

NG: *What does the story team do?*

KR: The story team, led by our story editor, take the raw material from the entire conference, which can be detailed or very, very broad, and then talk it through and iron out any problems and interrogate any flaws in the story and come out at the end of about two weeks' work with a document that is very precise. The document includes the episode number, transmission date, sets we've got, time of sunrise, sunset, production information, information on the characters that are being used and any information on the characters – for example, that one actor is on holiday, so we mustn't use him even if we want to. A document with 15 episodes written out like that is sent out to the writers and obviously an individual writer is assigned to each episode and then they have a few days with it. What we ask them to do is structure the episode from that storyline.

NG: *Explain how the writer structures the episode from the storyline?*

KR: The writer takes ownership of the structure as well as to an extent the content. The writers are welcome to come back on this storyline and say 'OK, I know what you need from me and I know where I'm picking up and I know what I've got to have to hand over on the moment for the next writer but I'd like to play things slightly differently across this episode.' They'll give us a suggestion of how they want to do it – for example, they might say: 'Can I have a couple of extra characters because I want to do this.' Sometimes they'll trade and say: 'I don't need so-and-so and I don't need so-and-so, but please can I have these two extra characters instead because I think they are more important for the story I need to tell.'

NG: *What happens at the commissioning conference?*

KR: When we come back for the next story conference, the first thing we do on the first morning is have a commissioning conference where all the writers sit round the table with the same producer and story editor and effectively sign off on their plans for their episodes. So they've submitted in writing the changes they want to make but then we'll talk them through, and again it is that kind of collective responsibility – collective ownership. A writer might say: 'OK, I want to play this slightly differently and you've said that X happens but I would like Y to happen but I've spoken to the person who is taking on the next episode and they are fine if I do Y. They'll pick it up in a slightly different way and we can assure you that by the end of that episode we'll be absolutely back to where you want us to be.' Or: 'We're going to do it differently all of us and it's going to be better.' We have that discussion and we agree or disagree. I mean, ultimately the producer has to make the call. It is a three-week cycle and that happens 17 times a year because of Christmas, and it's a 52-week year and there's one where we do it across a four-week cycle and we have to make up the extra episodes somewhere across the year. So that is the process. The writers leave the conference and they go away and write their first drafts.

NG: *What about the actual scriptwriting schedule?*

KR: We expect those episodes back as first drafts within about ten days. They have typically two to three weeks after that to take it through two more drafts. The big changes, if they're required, will happen after the first draft when it is just the producer and the script team talking it through and having read all the episodes around: continuity issues, places where the story isn't working, or something about the script they feel needs changing. The second draft goes to a production meeting. The director will join the process and obviously have his or her own notes. At that point we will have people looking at location; the script supervisor is looking at the timings and the various practical issues to take into account. The first assistant director will have got a draft schedule together. So when all that information is added into a second draft you come out with what we call a rehearsal script, which is only a third draft and usually that's fine and we shoot that. Sometimes we need a fourth draft. It is very unusual. It is a very efficient process, but what I think is really important about it is that we make most of the important decisions before the writer starts writing.

NG: *You've spoke about the three voices of* Coronation Street. *What are they? Voice 1?*

KR: I think there are three voices the writer has to capture if they are going to be successful. The first is the obvious one, the voices of all the characters – to get them right. Some of them are really easy and some of them are quite tricky. We'll tell them that Steve Macdonald will make such and such a decision on such and such a day, but the way they express Steve Macdonald is about the skill of capturing that character's voice. They have to be able to capture voices of all of our characters and do it convincingly.

NG: *And Voice 2?*

KR: Now the second voice the writer has to capture is a little harder to define but I think it's every bit as important and that is the voice of the programme. I think it was a voice that was laid down in the very clear blueprint by creator Tony Warren in Episode 1 and it's bit difficult to sum up in a few words but let me try. Obviously, it is dramatic but it's absolutely character-led drama and it's female-centric, character-led drama, and however dramatic and dark and gritty sometimes stories can be, there is an essential warmth and there is an essential humour that is laced through everything. It is not about we have a scene of drama and then we cut to a scene of comedy and that's kind of easy to do and less satisfactory. It's about the comedy and the drama being so closely intertwined that they're almost indistinguishable.

NG: *And Voice 3?*

KR: I think it is very important that the writer doesn't lose their own voice. I would never want all the *Coronation Street* scripts to sound and feel the same. Of course we've got issues of continuity and we're telling stories and we mustn't suddenly go off track, but I think when a writer brings out their own voice in an episode they do it in a particular way. Some of our writers have got very distinctive voices like Jonathan Harvey, Carmel Morgan, Jan McVerry, Joe Turner and Simon Crowther. They are telling the story that we want them to tell, but there is something of them in it as well. I think that is really important as well. So the challenge of working in the machine and capturing those three voices I think is considerable and it isn't just about being a great writer. It's about being able to do all of that.

NG: *Given that the show is high volume. Is there a problem with scripts being rewritten?*

KR: Very rarely. It may happen once or twice a year out of 260-odd episodes that we get to the point where the script is totally not working and something's gone badly wrong with it and you just think the only solution to this is to start again because the individual writer has run up against a brick wall. It just happens. It is part of the creative process. It's not that writer is useless; it is just that there is a problem now. Then you say: 'Right, let's just start again and we're going to ask someone else to take a fresh look at this because the script's just not working.'

NG: *What are the common, avoidable mistakes in a* Coronation Street *script?*

KR: I think there are two sorts of common mistakes: doing too much of something or not enough of something. Let me expand on that. I think, for example, in characterization I think it is very easy to overdraw the characters and exaggerate their traits to the point where they are cartoons rather than real, rounded people. Equally, it's a common mistake that all the characters sound very bland and are interchangeable. You do this test where you block out the characters' names and then you read the dialogue. Can you actually tell who's speaking? If you can't, then that's wrong. You shouldn't need the character headings above the speeches to be able to hear which character it is. I think similarly in terms of their overall approach to the storytelling. A common mistake would be to stick so slavishly to what we've given them that the overall episode feels voiceless in terms of the writer's own voice. Or to go so far off piste that actually it's all very interesting but these aren't the stories we're telling.

NG: *For a new writer to join the show presumably, like any other job, there has to be a vacancy? Do you have a pool of writers-in-waiting as such?*

KR: Perhaps if one writer left the team we wouldn't be rushing into it, but if we lost two writers then I think that's the point we'd say 'OK, who else is out there?' We tend to have a list of writers who are queuing up to join the show. It tends to work like that and they range from very well-established writers to people who don't have any television credits but who have a passion, and sometimes those people can work out but obviously they have to work harder to prove themselves. So we tend not to need to go out and find writers. They come and find us.

NG: *Do they need to be fans of the show?*

KR: I don't think they need to be. I think it helps. It helps if they at least have knowledge of the history of the characters, the stories we've played and some knowledge of the kind of stories that work on *Coronation Street.* I think there's an argument that says they also need a degree of critical detachment. If they are too much of a fan, they are possibly not going to be able to make the right decisions. What I think would be very difficult, to turn that on its head, is if someone came to us who was a very good writer but really didn't appear to have any interest in *Coronation Street*, who didn't know about our characters or the history of our stories. I would then think I don't really see how they are going to get passionate about the next Ken and Deidre story.

Doctors

Doctors is the BBC's daytime soap that goes out five days a week in the early afternoon. The show, launched in 2000, is about the lives of the staff and patients at the fictional Mill Health Centre. Since the show began more than 2,000 episodes have been broadcast and the production team currently produces 236 episodes a year.

The show has a proud record of giving writers their first on-screen credit. *Doctors* has been described as a continuing drama with a soap element. Each episode focuses on the 'story of the day', with a couple of character-driven serial elements as well. It is up to the writers to pitch, either verbally or written down, stories of the day and, if the editorial team like one, the writer will be commissioned to write the episode.

The story of the day will have guest characters at its heart but will be linked in some way to one of the regular cast members who have to be integral to that story. Writers often have preferences for their favourite characters and tend to utilize them for their story of the day.

A writer may also pitch a multi-episode story told over two, three or more episodes. On other occasions the serial element involving the regular characters may take centre stage and the commissioned writer will be given a storyline document – as on *EastEnders* or *Coronation Street* – and present the serial story as they see fit.

Doctors is a daytime drama and as such has a smaller budget and much smaller cast of characters to draw upon. In turn, there are limitations on locations and guest characters as well as limitations imposed by regular character availability.

The show also works to the adage of 'Don't let reality get in the way of a good story' and liberties are taken with the real world. In the real world, for example, doctors don't do house calls and test results are not immediate. Dramatic licence wins the day and the audience goes with it.

Most writers joining *Doctors* will undergo a trial script first. The writer will be presented with a pack containing maps of the surgeries, character biographies and guidelines for the show – for example, each episode averages a maximum 30 scenes. Even though it is a trial script the writer still needs to pitch a story of the day that will take up the majority of the episode. Once the story of the day has been accepted, the writer is presented with a document containing the serial element. Two strands of serial storyline are presented in a single paragraph form for each story which contains a handful of story beats which will carry the story from the previous episode to the end-of-episode cliffhanger.

The writer's job is to weave the serial element into their story of the day. A scene-by-scene is written and may go through several drafts before being signed off, and the script is written with a limited number of drafts before it goes into production.

EastEnders

EastEnders is the BBC's only primetime soap and it goes out on weekdays four times a week and is regularly the BBC's most watched drama. Launched in 1985, the show is about the residents of the fictional London borough of Walford.

Note: The BBC also produces two other soaps – *River City* in Scotland and the Welsh-language *Pobol y Cwm* for S4C in Wales.

Bryan Kirkwood *was executive producer of* EastEnders *from 2010 to 2012 where he oversaw approximately 400 episodes. He had previously been executive producer on Channel 4's* Hollyoaks *for 346 episodes. This interview took place during Bryan's tenure on the show.*

Nicholas Gibbs: *How many writers do you have working on* EastEnders?

Bryan Kirkwood: We have a core team of roughly ten people and it is the core team that attends the monthly story meetings and attends our long-term conferences and whose job it is to find the next big stories and keep the engine running and going in the right direction. Beyond that core team we have another roughly 20 people who regularly contribute by writing episodes and are very much still very important creative influences on the show.

NG: *How do you source your new writers for the show?*

BK: We have a number of avenues. I am very keen to create and maintain a consistency on the *EastEnders* writing team. There are always opportunities for new talent and that's right because it is the BBC. We should be seen and it is part of our job to create opportunities for exciting new talent. Balancing that, it is very important to me to have a consistency to the creative energy to the show. In terms of new writers, we have a couple of avenues. First there's the trial scheme. We have a development editor who is charged with always trying to find new writers. You will always be juggling a number of writers doing trial scripts, which has borne fruit in the past and certainly some of our current writers have come through that route. We have John Yorke's brilliant Writers' Academy, which has proved enormously successful in finding these brilliant new voices who are now central to the voice of *EastEnders* such as Matt Evans, Sally Abbott and Lauren Clee – three writers off the top of my head who have been through John's Academy scheme. Then the other, less structured way is through all of us who work here – we all come from different shows, we all come from different backgrounds in the television industry, and you know, if you work with a good writer and you feel they are right for *EastEnders*, then that's another way in.

NG: *When you look at a writer's original script what do you look for that suggests they could be an* EastEnders *writer?*

BK: *EastEnders* is a very difficult show to write. It has got a very unique voice. What I would look for in a writer is the confidence to have their own voice while still sounding resolutely like *EastEnders*. I think we have some of the best characters on British television with Dot Cotton, with Kat and Alfie Moon, with Ian Beale and Phil Mitchell... the list goes on. We have very, very distinct characters who have been on screen for many, many years and so one of the first things I would look for in a potential writer is: Have they got the joy of those characters right? Have they got wit? Have they got banter? Is it entertaining? It's a very simple question but am I enjoying this episode? Am I enjoying the characters? Do I want to turn the page? It's always too much of a danger to rely on telling a story through words and I would look for the ability to tell these stories visually. Sometimes on a show like *EastEnders* there is nothing better than two people talking in a room. That's got a lot going for it. That's what the show is built on. Sometimes, though, it is better to tell it visually so I look for a balance of that as well. I look for confidence, I look for structure. I look for rhythm, I look for pace. Am I bored? Has the writer enjoyed writing it? I can usually tell if it has been a labour of love or a labour.

NG: *With those iconic characters such as Phil Mitchell is there a fine line between nailing that character and going into caricature?*

BK: Yes, absolutely. I mean interestingly the character of Janine is one of our larger-than-life characters. She is very colourful but sometimes when I read a script by an aspiring *EastEnders* writer Janine is written like a pantomime queen. So there is absolutely a danger that, in pursuing the uniqueness of the character voice, they can slip into caricature, and that is something to look out for.

What is unique about this show is the obviously often heard but slightly unfortunate tag of *EastEnders* being depressing and I would always be looking for a writer to challenge that tag. The show is not predisposed to be negative and sometimes I think new writers feel that is the role they've got to perform and I will always challenge that.

NG: *What sort of things do you hate seeing in an episode of* EastEnders*?*

BK: Avoid self-pity in the characters. We don't always get this right. It's about that classic British kind of strength of character based on the Blitz spirit. Our show should be about our characters' survival – their spirit and their ambition survives. Their aspirations are in a resolutely working-class environment but I would always ask us to strive towards positivity and have them making the best of their situation.

NG: *When a writer joins the show, what is the induction process?*

BK: What would happen is the writer would attend a monthly meeting. Once a month the core writers meet and talk about the next month's set of episodes. A new writer might attend that monthly meeting to get up to speed with where we are in stories, obviously because we would be a month ahead of them to what has been transmitted at the time. They will be assigned a script editor who they will work very closely with throughout the process. They'll get to know that script editor very well and it's a friendly face, someone on the end of the phone. They are given a commissioning document which is every episode across that month period and also given previous commissioning documents in order to get up to speed with what stories we're telling. After that there's a mammoth amount of homework: they are given their three-page episode document featuring their A story, their B story and couple of other supporting stories. Now I would always task the writer to make that content their own. They have got to interrogate that information and challenge it, ask questions and, if they don't like it, then come up with something better. And if they don't believe in it, then ask why they don't believe in it. What they must do is ask every single question of themselves and of the story team before they type a word.

NG: *How long does a writer get to work on their episode?*

BK: It is a balanced and well-oiled machine. From the commissioning conference, where we discuss the changes they have to make to their episode, what to keep, what's got to change, what to tweak so that it works across the continuity of the whole block. Then, with everything signed off, the writer is in full possession of the facts with what they are about to write. They have roughly about two weeks to go away and write their first draft. If they are later in the block in weeks 2, 3 and 4, they have a bit longer. After the first draft is delivered and, depending where they are in the block, a week or so later we will meet collectively – myself, the script editor and a couple of my editorial colleagues will meet and we'll discuss that week's episodes of first drafts.

On *EastEnders* after the first draft you're given notes. The writer delivers a second draft about a week or so later, then there is another meeting which the director comes in on and that becomes very much a live production. That's when the director starts visualizing, wardrobe, design, the props... the whole production starts moving at the second draft. And so it is much more difficult at that stage making anything other than small changes. Another two further drafts where hopefully all is going well; the notes will be about spelling, typos, long-term character continuity and scheduling.

NG: *What about rewriting by script editors?*

BK: It never happens. I'm extremely tough on the idea of that. I think it is the wrong thing to happen, the wrong thing to do and I always insist that, if something isn't working, the script editor goes back to the writer. If things are falling apart, which they occasionally do – and I'm told it happens much less now than it used to on *EastEnders* – for any number of reasons, it doesn't work out with a particular writer. It could simply be the wrong writer with the wrong episode. We have to make a judgement call early on in the process to relieve the writer of the episode and recommission it.

NG: *Like any other job, for you to take on somebody else there has to be a vacancy. What is the writer turnover? Is there an extended pool to call on?*

BK: I would be foolish to turn down a brilliant writer for *EastEnders* – that's a fact. They have to be brilliant. It's what's at stake. Whether they are brand new or whether they've got 30 years' experience, I don't care. I'd be delighted to welcome someone who has never written for television before, but if they have come through the correct entry system by the trial, by John's Writers' Academy, and if they are up to the job, then brilliant – welcome! That said, we only have a set number of episodes a year, and we already have a number of writers on the team. Inevitably, there will be some writers who want a holiday or extended break for six months off to write for another show or writers who think they have done their time and want to go somewhere else. So there is some movement on the edges of the team.

NG: *Do writers need to be fans of* EastEnders *or do they need to do their homework?*

BK: I'd say they do need to be a fan of the show. It is a labour of love. To be honest, I don't know why you would write for the show if you didn't love it. You have got to love every character. We have some very uncompromising characters and again, if you come to write for the show believing the worst of its reputation, I don't think it is going to benefit anyone, least of all the writer and certainly not the audience.

Emmerdale

ITV's *Emmerdale* is the most prolific soap on British television, producing an incredible six episodes a week. The show debuted in 1972 and is set in the fictional Yorkshire village of *Emmerdale*.

Tony Hammond *knows the show inside out, having joined the show in 2003, and has worked as a script editor, a storyliner, story producer, script producer and assistant producer.*

Nicholas Gibbs: *For the three people who don't know, what is* Emmerdale?

Tony Hammond: *Emmerdale* is a six-times-a-week rural serial drama (soap opera). We commonly use the term 'small village, big drama', which hopefully gives the best impression of what we are trying to create with our show.

NG: *How many writers work on* Emmerdale*? How many are core writers?*

TH: We currently have a team of 23 core writers. Over the years this has fluctuated between 19 and 25 writers, depending on the producer's vision for the show. All writers who work on the show are considered core team.

NG: *How do you source new writers for the show?*

TH: Obviously, we are contacted by agents all the time who advertise their clients and some writers have been successful in this route. We source new writers from all areas. Predominantly, we search for writers with proven past drama experience. Many of our writers have written for other dramas and soaps but we do also consider writers who have solely written for theatre and/or radio etc. A few writers have progressed from the story and script offices also.

NG: *What would you look for in the writer's original script that would suggest to you and your team that the writer could potentially write for* Emmerdale*?*

TH: When a writer sends in their unsolicited script there is a select team of script readers on *Emmerdale* whose job is to filter the scripts depending on their writing skills and then recommend whether we should consider sending them a trial script to work on. The filtering system works on the fundamental premise that we want to be entertained by the dialogue and most people fall short, as their dialogue is sometimes too mundane. We look for truthful, natural, emotional and characterful speeches. While not essential, having watched the show and knowing the characters is very useful.

NG: *When a writer joins the show, what is the induction process and the guidance they are given to be an* Emmerdale *writer?*

TH: As we usually employ writers with proven experience of writing drama, there's not really any guidance they are given in terms of writing for the show. Practically, though, they are given a writer's pack which includes basic biogs and maps and character information they will need to write their episodes. We also give them a tour of both the studio sets and location sets to familiarize themselves with the characters' surroundings.

NG: *What is the process, from the writing point of view, of an* Emmerdale *episode? What information is the writer given to write an episode?*

TH: Each writer is given a storyline document which provides the basic beats. Each storyline usually has four to six stories involving a specific number of characters. Writers are expected to structure their own episodes and provide a basic outline of their proposed episode to be discussed at commissioning. Writers also have access to our in-house researcher and archivist who can provide information to help make the story as truthful as possible.

NG: *Are the core writers part of the storylining team or does* Emmerdale *have separate storyliners from the writing team?*

TH: We have a separate team of six storyliners led by a story editor who write and provide the storyline document for the writers to base their episode on.

NG: *From commission to delivery, what is the timescale for an* Emmerdale *script?*

TH: It takes approximately four to five months in total from commissioning through to seeing the episode transmitted on air. A single script goes through a three-month process of editing before hitting the production teams for filming and editing.

NG: *What are the benefits of writing for* Emmerdale *to a writer's career?*

TH: I believe a serial drama is a great career for any writer. Most writers tend to see it as a massive learning curve due to the amount of writing and crafting a single episode takes and the speed at which they have to do it. Some writers do see writing for soap to be a stepping stone to greater things, but I know many writers who are happy to stay in the genre and earn a very decent crust from it.

NG: *What makes a good* Emmerdale *script?*

TH: A good balance of light and dark stories mixed with humour and emotion, combined with brilliant pace and structure and drama! Overall, it needs to be a bloody good entertaining read!

NG: *What are the common, avoidable mistakes in* Emmerdale *scripts?*

TH: Mundane dialogue. It might be realistic but would you yourself want to watch two people discussing 'how many sugars'? Also, writers must remember they are writing for a visual medium. It's not purely about the words but also the actions and showing and not always telling. On a personal level – clichés are the bane of my life. Also, I hate the words 'anyway', 'just', and the phrases 'what's going on?' and 'of course'.

NG: *To what extent, if any, does rewriting take place by the head writer or script editor?*

TH: We rarely rewrite writers' work. Only in emergencies when the writer is unavailable will we tweak and fiddle with dialogue. From *Emmerdale*'s perspective the writer is the auteur and takes full responsibility for every word and full stop in their script.

NG: *Do you associate particular writers with particular characters? That is, if it is a certain character-centric episode, is there a preference for a particular writer to write that episode?*

TH: The simple answer to this is yes. Obviously, all episodes have lots of different characters in it so writers need to know each voice and how they would react to write a truthful script. However, there is obviously an A story in each episode and certain writers do have more of a connection to certain characters. So, where possible, we try to place writers on episodes which we feel they will write the best. Sometimes this boils down to the specific characters which feature in the episode, but this can also be based on the story and tone of the episode. Some writers are more comfortable with darker stories whereas some are better at comedic stories.

NG: *For a new writer to join the show presumably, like any other job, there has to be a vacancy? Do you have a pool of writers-in-waiting as such?*

TH: To a certain extent, there has to be a vacancy – we can't take on a limitless number of writers as budget does come into the equation. We tend not to keep writers waiting for vacancies as it can take a very long time for the core team to change and it would be unfair and soul-destroying for the writer to be kept dangling in the hope of a slot arising. There have been occasions where we have been interested in taking on a writer but our schedules and their schedules just did not match up and therefore unfortunately it didn't work out.

NG: *Do writers need to be a fan of* Emmerdale *to join the show?*

TH: I would never say we never take on writers who haven't watched the show as I'd be fearful of missing the next big thing. However, as with most shows, I would presume, having knowledge of the show would put you in good stead for getting a job writing on it. It's certainly one of the first questions I always ask writers who approach us or whom I meet at events.

Hollyoaks

Channel 4's *Hollyoaks*, produced by Lime Pictures, is a five-night youth drama that was created by Phil Redmond and set in the fictional Cheshire suburb of Hollyoaks.

Emma Smithwick, a former scriptwriter and script supervisor on the BBC teen soap, The Cut, *joined the* Hollyoaks *script department before becoming the show's series producer in 2011.*

Nicholas Gibbs: *What is* Hollyoaks?

Emma Smithwick: What I am aiming for is *Hollyoaks* to be more of a youth drama than a soap. I think possibly it would be fair to differentiate *Hollyoaks* from any other soap by saying what I am after is real, emotional integrity and character development. I think our audience can be anaesthetized if you just keep throwing masses of storylines and story plot without really rooting it in character. That's what I want *Hollyoaks* to be.

NG: *How do you source your writers?*

ES: In a number of different ways. A lot of agents come to me with established soap writers. I also look at Edinburgh Fringe or see as many plays as I can. For me, we have such well-established soap hands on this show that do such a brilliant job but there is something special about getting brand-new writers. Since I've been here there has been about ten brand-new writers getting their first ever credit. So, while we need the experience, it is quite nice to look for brand-new writers and they come from anywhere. There are big brands I will look at like *E20* or *Skins*. To me, they fit in straight away with what we are trying to do with *Hollyoaks* or looking at brand-new writers like Daniel Moven. He is 19 and he just sent in his scripted authored piece. It made me laugh. It needed work structurally. You can tell by reading it that he wasn't experienced but he got that immediate authenticity and the voice I'm looking for. Similarly, another girl, Marnie Dickens, got her first ever TV credit when she did a spec script for *Hollyoaks*. It was terrific.

NG: *How does your shadow script scheme work?*

ES: Writers come to conference and we ask them if they liked to pitch, which can be incredibly daunting when you're coming into a very established show. Most of them come in armed with a pitch which is brilliant. Then I will, depending on their experience, put them straight onto a broadcast trial. So their trial script will be a broadcast episode because I feel confident in their writing. I feel confident in the support network we have here to mould them to a place when they can get a broadcast opportunity. Then with other writers perhaps I might feel like that they should do a shadow trial and they will shadow somebody and they will deliver a script. They will all go to at least one conference before they get a commission.

NG: *What is the timeframe from commission to delivery?*

ES: The timeframe in the conference is three days and they finish on the Friday and a week later we ask for a scene-by-scene after commissioning. It's two weeks to deliver their first draft from commissioning. Then from first draft to second draft about eight days; then another three to five days for the producer, director; then another three or four days for a shooting script – that's about five, six weeks. From conference it is about eight weeks. In conference, we actually say to the writer here is your episode.

NG: *Are they given character and set availability in advance?*

ES: The Friday after conference they send in the Character Emotional Journeys only and a week later they send in their Scene Breakdown. Our story team – we've got a story associate and a story producer –

who take in all their emotional breakdowns to make sure that it all tallies and that they don't have any repeat beats. Then they send them back out to the writers with their character lists, character counts. We usually don't do locations because we will work that out in Scene Breakdowns.

NG: *How are emotional breakdowns presented?*

ES: They are presented in a paragraph and they are coloured up in their strands and it is the main protagonist in each of the main story strands but it is just emotional. Basically, where they start off in their episode and where they leave them off. So we can be sure of the dynamics journey for them.

NG: *Do writers ever get rewritten on* Hollyoaks?

ES: It takes a lot for me to resubmit something to get somebody else to do it. I think a lot of that comes from the fact that I was a writer and you really should be given the opportunity to make it better. If you really can't, then you concede 'well OK'. We have to be so up against the deadlines to bring on somebody else.

NG: *Are there things you don't want to see on* Hollyoaks?

ES: I think I'm pretty much open to most things actually. There is very little that I'll just say no to. Two things perhaps: one is the irresponsible storyteller. For me, and maybe this comes from the fact that I started at the BBC as a career where the audience to me is my first concern. The audience that we cater for is 16 to 24 and have a wide spectrum. I also think our audience looks at a show like this almost as an emotional encyclopaedia. It's kind of real-life learning in many respects. Every storyline I consider has an absolute duty to the audience. So irresponsible storytelling such as encouraging our audience to do things that I just don't believe are right, without getting worthy or dictating how someone should be. That's one thing I'm against. The other thing is unnecessary smoking, taking drugs; it's not just compliance for Channel 4, but in general. In terms of style, as a long as every writer that comes to the show really wants to write for this audience and has a passion for storytelling. Above all it's the storytelling. When you meet people, meet writers, meet directors, you kind of know instantly whether they bounce off this audience. I think it is the most exciting audience to deliver for because they are not going to hang around. They haven't developed habits. They are not *Guardian* readers, *Telegraph* readers. They are very channel and platform blind. They don't care how they consume it or where they consume it. It is just a good show or it's not a good show. So for me that's hugely challenging but as long as my writers and my directors know that's the mark they have to hit every time I'm open to any subject, any form of storytelling; in fact, the more unconventional the better. I think it is all in the planning as well. It can be as a sophisticated as a story as you want it to be but it has got to be prepped.

NG: *Do writers need to be the fan of the show? Or at least* become *a fan of the show?*

ES: When they first join the show they don't need to be a fan of the show necessarily. They need to very quickly engage with the show and enjoy who they are writing for. I think if I made that a prerequisite I'd be drawing from quite a small pool at the moment because I think the show could afford to be more intelligent, wittier, more sophisticated. I want to make *Hollyoaks* a destination for writers and for directors creatively. Not just to put on a show, not just to get their foot in the door, but a lot of writers that we have are still passionate about the show and you can tell that when they write; you can tell when they pitch and that is a breath of fresh air. So for me the prerequisite is that they have to be passionate about the audience.

NG: *Does that mean writers need to be younger-skewing?*

ES: One of things I did in conference was to ask everybody to bring in a photo of themselves when they were a teenager and to put it on the *Hollyoaks* writers' wall of shame. When I did that it was to say to everybody in the room that everybody is qualified to write for this audience because everybody in that room has been that audience at one time. Being 16, 17, you know, it's shit being a teenager. Sometimes these saccharin and glossy American shows make it look so cool and so effortless but it's not. And we'll keep talking about that and just remembering. The *Hollyoaks* I want to be the producer of is the one that tells the story that the smaller things in life are actually the biggest.

NG: *What advice would you give writers?*

ES: It's just doing it. I think the most useful thing I think is reading scripts. I really do. I don't think because of deadlines you can get caught up in a soap bubble when you're writing for a soap and quite quickly it can become navel-gazing. I think if you watch other TV dramas and read the scripts it just works offering more ideas. That's really important. In terms of getting a writing job, I think it's a case of being really brave, and if there is a show you really want to write for it's just finding a way in at any level. There are a lot of people who come into our script department for work experience. They'll come in and ask me if they can come into conference or they'll ask if they can come in for a first draft and sometimes they'll pipe up with a brilliant idea and totally solve the story problem. They'll just be brave and they'll be tenacious.

One thing I wish somebody had pointed out to me and it may seem an obvious one, but knowing the world of your story and remembering what it's like to be our audience watching it. I could read a script, take the writer's name off it and know who it is by the detail they add in; they've watched all the back episodes, they know the world they're dealing with. Once you've got that, it's half the battle because then you just close your eyes and know where you are and know what's going on around you. You've got so many characters to think of, but if you're in that world it will come quite naturally and that's the same for every show I think.

Casualty

Casualty is the world's longest-running medical drama about the staff and patients of the accident and emergency department of Holby General Hospital. It goes out in primetime every Saturday night on BBC1. It first opened its doors in 1986.

Nicola Larder *was script producer and producer on the show from 2010 to 2012. She had previously been a script editor and script executive on* New Tricks *and produced a two-part mini-series,* Mister Eleven. *In 2012 she joined* Waterloo Road *as a producer.*

Nicholas Gibbs: *What kind of show is* Casualty?

Nicola Larder: When it was originally greenlit it was because of the uniqueness of having a central male nurse. It was more politically driven. It was about the NHS and its existence. Nowadays it is a popular piece of primetime entertainment, not least because of its competition. We are always up against *The X-Factor* or *Britain's Got Talent*.

NG: *What makes a good* Casualty *episode?*

NL: Well, we've a new exec, Jonathan Young, take over and we've asked ourselves that question: What makes a good episode? We've returned to a lot of the core values. Our audience are happy when they are able to enjoy a damn fine stunt. They like the feeling of the anticipation of something going very wrong and they like, more than anything, the two very strong, self-contained guest stories. They tune in, our audience, on average one out of three episodes. They don't tune in for the soap element – i.e. the continuing relationships, trials and tribulations of the regular doctors – although the audience, according to research, are, in particular, huge fans of Jordan and huge fans of Charlie.

So that is what they like – the self-contained element of the patient guest stories – and when it is at its best those stories are well targeted at the core demographic and our core audience. They are well told, with a beginning, middle and end, and are emotionally absorbing, with high stakes and with a very natural integrated use of medicine. We tend to create scenarios – writers will tend to pitch guest story ideas which naturally integrate medicine, albeit they won't have technical detail but they will say how the story is going to fit in very nicely with your two bits of serial drama that we're going to give you. So what happens is you might have an episode where you've got Zoe and Jordan's relationship becoming more intimate, for argument's sake, and below that Linda struggles to deal with her new boss. So the writer is given those and they have to find a way to tell those stories well and in a way which will naturally integrate themselves into their own original creations. A writer should never be literal and say, because Linda is struggling with her boss, we are going to have a guest story with somebody struggling with their boss who gets into an accident. You should feel that the whole episode is a cohesive, harmonious whole –therefore, what story is going to highlight Linda's dilemma of the week? What other guest stories are going to highlight Zoe and Jordan's dilemma that week?

NG: *Is the process that writers come with guest stories first or do you present them with the serial element stories first?*

NL: It's a 12-week development process from the writers being commissioned to the script being delivered as a shooting script. The writers within a 12-episode run will all be given one central story document and that will cover Episodes 1 to 12. They will look at what episodes they are writing and look at the serial story they've got to cover. They'll be a couple of paragraphs on each. There might a line about other characters they have to feature: like Lenny is in a bad mood because he has been assigned to cubicles; Tom is enjoying working with the nurses. So they'll get that and off the back of that the writers will come in and pitch their ideas for guest stories and very broadly speaking we like to work in a five-act structure.

You'll pitch it and it is something that is wonderful and personal but exciting to you as a writer. So you pitch ideas and then the team work with you to develop that to five acts and then, within two weeks of that original commissioning meeting, you then have to deliver a scene-by-scene. Once that's signed off, you then have to deliver within two weeks your first draft. You work on three or four more drafts to take you through to production. Off the back of the production draft you then have the medical meeting. After the medical notes the shooting script is released within a week of the shoot.

NG: *In terms of an episode, what are the practical constraints – for example, what actors are available, how many outdoor locations are allowed, etc.?*

NL: You do have to impose some restrictions. You have to create these scripts with an eye for them being feasible to actually go into production. We always want to block two shooting blocks simultaneously. You are given restrictions according to cross-scheduling with another unit. So if you have Jordan and Zoe in an A story, your parallel block won't have Jordan and Zoe in an A story;

otherwise you will need them in two places at once to shoot the majority of the scenes. So the story document helps diminish the likelihood of getting notes like: 'Can you change the main actor because the other unit needs them?'

NG: *So the writer would get that from the outset – these are the actors available etc.?*

NL: If it's not from the outset, it is quite early on in the development. You are also given a guide which tells you approximately how many pages of your script can be set on location, how many pages of your script need to be set in Studio A and then how many pages of your script need to be set in Studio B. For argument's sake, let's say 15 per cent is generally speaking where your accident is going to happen away from the hospital. Studio A is pretty much all of our hospital set: it's the reception area, it's resus, it's cubicles, it's the admin area where the nurses are, staff rooms, the family room where the bad news is delivered. That's really where you are going to be shooting the majority of your episodes. Studio B is an extra set which is called CDU – the Clinical Decisions Unit - and that's a big ward or Exterior ED [Emergency Department]. I actually think it is quite good fun as a writer to work within those parameters – it kind of harnesses how you tell stories. You can tell the same story a million different ways but if you know you've got these parameters it enables you to focus on the most precise way of telling your story. You are given, at the moment, seven guest characters to play with, so if you split that across two guest stories, two are patients and the rest are people's friends, relations, perpetrators.

NG: *So it is after the first draft that the harsh practicality of being able to do it comes into play?*

NL: We shoot an episode of *Casualty* in ten days. That's generally speaking Monday to Friday – five days of it in the studio, two days of it are in CDU or ED and three days are on location. We work within tight budgets so there's no point in encouraging the writer to write something that is never shootable. We create good relationships with our writers so before you begin you have a conversation about what we are able to do. We take you round the set. We show you how you can write an episode with flow and groove. I'll always make the things that are important to the story a priority and those that might not necessarily need to be part of the story I'll ask that writer to compromise on and we'll negotiate.

NG: *Where do you source your writers?*

NL: Well, we have eight episodes already allotted thanks to the Writers' Academy. They obviously got their own process for choosing all those writers. So that's eight out of 42 or 48 episodes a year. We have core writers, the numbers of which fluctuate and they'll write between three or four. There are commissioned episodic writers and that can be through our Shadow Scheme writers. In 2011, we took ten writers because we've got an initiative at the moment which will evolve year-on-year to encourage local talent to write for the show. We got some extra funding to enable some Welsh writers to come on (*Casualty* is made in Cardiff, Wales). I think we had ten. We also get lots of ideas from agents. Every single person who submits a piece of work to the show has their script read by one or two members of the editorial team. Everyone gets feedback on their script. Everyone on the Shadow Scheme writes a version of a *Casualty* but everyone else will submit something from their slate, albeit something that has been transmitted or something they've developed.

NG: *Where someone submits an original piece of work, what element do you see that suggests they can write for* Casualty?

NL: Generally speaking, it is wise to look for a full-length script, for something that is a transmittable hour of TV. Half-hour scripts are always going to pose questions about whether a writer is able to plot across a longer form or not. You want to see that writing x factor – good writing. You want to see not only a compelling plot and compelling story but that this writer can create rounded, three-dimensional exciting characters with a joy that makes you read. It's like anything – you want to feel: 'That's not hard to read.'

NG: *Are those the people, then, whom you don't feel you can give a direct commission, so you guide them to the Shadow Scheme?*

NL: Not necessarily. I commissioned a writer off the back of having read his *Shameless* script, which is a completely different show. It's Channel 4. It's post-watershed. It's subversive. It's sexual. It was a really, really good script. I invited him to meet us and he knew about *Casualty*. He talked about it. We exchanged ideas on it. He'd engaged in the show, and so any writer who wants to write on any show needs to be well prepared. So one should watch it weekly and should watch a run of it because you can't really get the measure of a show by just seeing one episode. The thing is with *Casualty* you can never say it's not on. It is always on. It was a combination of me being excited by his writing samples and then being excited about what he had to say about the show which meant that he got taken on a commission. It has also worked in reverse. I've got excited about a writing sample and invited the writer in and they have had so little knowledge of the show and you think 'Really?' That's not the best. I don't want encyclopaedic knowledge because you begin to grow that the more involved in the show you are.

NG: So the writers come through the Writers' Academy, Shadow Scheme, and submissions via agents?

NL: We do get unsolicited material. It is very rare to have a writer that is not represented or commissioned. I think: they've got through the process of competitively seeking an agent, who is a quality control already in part. Writers most certainly don't have to have a transmitted television credit to get a commission on *Casualty*, although it is very helpful, particularly as *Casualty* is very challenging to write.

NG: *What about rewriting?*

NL: Well, it is something that we try to avoid and, therefore, it is something that only happens *in extremis*. We have every intention of getting the majority of writers who are commissioned through. The reasons it happens can be manifold. It is not something that we want to do and rewriting doesn't exist within the editorial team. Rewriting involves the writer being let go and the reasons being explained and then another writer is commissioned to replace them.

NG: Casualty *often opens on a big event. How do you maintain the pace so you've got somewhere to go?*

NL: It's interesting. What we advise the writers is that they don't structure the A and the B story in an identical way. So the A story will have its own five-act structure as will the B story. It doesn't mean that both patients are attacked or involved in accidents at the same point simultaneously. They don't degenerate simultaneously. Running the two stories out of sync will mean when one hits high the other can rest and vice versa... What you want to do is to use your locations as creatively as possible. You don't have to use it all up at the start. You want to leave the hospital in the middle.

One thing writers need to consider is how grave the situation is in their A and B story. The problem is you can sometimes push yourself into making that person so poorly that a) they wouldn't realistically remain in the ED and b) they are unconscious so they can't say anything. So, you know, you use the medical advice and say, 'Well, you know I like them to be so ill here that they are going to need a procedure that we can perform in the ED. I would like by Act 4 for them to be able to regain consciousness and not look like we are entirely fabricating medicine.' So you want to hook the audience in at the top but you need to create reasons for them to keep engaging, so if all the excitement is top-loaded then there is something structurally wrong with the episode. If we have a moment's reprieve with the guest, then surely that's when something from the serial story could kick in – for example, where two of our doctors have an incredible disagreement. So it's about looking at every moment where you can to create a dilemma because as soon as everyone agrees the conflict dies and, therefore, the drama dies because drama is essentially about conflict. It's not always about arguments. It's about differing opinions.

Holby City

Holby City is the medical spin-off series from *Casualty*. The show hit the screens in 1999 and is set in the same hospital as *Casualty* but in the different departments of the surgical wards.

Simon Harper *is the show's script producer whose job includes searching for and developing new writers for the show. His role also includes being the senior script editor on the show and in 2011/12 he began producing episodes.*

NG: *How would you describe the show?*

SH: *Holby City* started as a spin-off to *Casualty* in 1999. It is a very different show from *Casualty*. Nominally, it is set in the same hospital but it is set in the surgical wards. *Holby* was designed as a surgical spin-off and as such is a different show. It is more American-style, almost glossier, slightly heightened. *Holby* characters are huge characters, quite heightened characters. So there is a different tone and aspiration to *Holby*. At the moment we define ourselves by what we call the four Hs – Head, Heart, Hooks and Humour. *Holby* should always feel smart. It should always feel heart. It should be intelligent. It is a show with a very strong female demographic. It should have emotionally driven stories that tug at the heart. It should have pace. A huge sea change, which is fundamental to the brand at the moment, that has been brought on board by Justin Young, our lead writer and series producer, is humour. You need an episode to have that organic character-driven humour to balance the meatier, more emotional strands, to be quite playful, have a twinkle, if you like. I believe that is a vital part of our tone and identity.

NG: *Where do you source your writers from for* Holby?

SH: All kinds of places. One gives out what I call straight commissions. A straight commission can mean that they have an existing body of work; they have got the credits of an hour-long broadcast drama on TV. So that is mostly how I commission. I also run yearly shadow schemes – all the continuing dramas run shadow schemes – I always run mine every autumn for about six writers. The scheme maybe for somebody who is much less experienced. Or maybe somebody is experienced but you're not entirely sure about them in terms of their fit with this particular show. It is all about fit for the show. You can be a very inexperienced writer and do the most brilliant *Holby* script ever. You could be the most incredibly experienced writer on any number of other shows but for some reason that marriage of tone, aspiration, characters, the world, the ease of writing about doctors realistically and about people at work, it may not work out. The point of the shadow scheme is people can try out in a safe, trial environment without the pressure of a real commission. The shadow scheme writers come in here for a day, I'll give them a lecture and immerse them in the world and most vitally the format of *Holby*, and they are sent off and paid a small sum of money to write a trial script, half a script. They write the A strand of a *Holby* script. A *Holby* script is three-pronged if you like, A being 50 per cent of the weight, B being 30 per cent and C being 20 per cent. Then you commission on the basis of what they've done. I had six writers on the shadow scheme last year and I commissioned four of them.

NG: *What do you look for in an original script?*

SH: I want to see quite clever and complex storytelling. I don't think people realize how challenging a *Holby* is to write. It is not just three strands of soap you're leaping between. It is 60 minutes, which is not ITV where you are essentially writing 42 minutes with ad breaks; it is not even *Casualty*, which is 50 minutes. You have got to fill a whole hour. It is like a mini-movie, which is a lot of material. Those three strands, the A, B and C story, are set on three different wards more often than not but they can't feel divergent. You can't just flip between them. They've not only got to be clever, non-linear stories in themselves which twist and turn and surprise us; they've got to intertwine and feel crafted and part of the whole. You're not just tuning into a soap; you are creating your own crafted one hour of primetime television on BBC1. It has got to be accordingly polished and crafted. I also look for very smart, sexy dialogue, another *Holby* must, and truthful but fresh-feeling characterization, as well as heart and humour.

NG: *What is the act structure to a* Holby City *episode?*

SH: In a way we work in very traditional film school acts – five acts, a protagonist, a quest, an obstacle to that quest – a formula that sits very naturally with medical drama. You set up in that Inciting Incident, in the first act, what they need, what they want, their call to arms, and the rest unfolds over a traditional five act structure of dream phase, obstacles, nightmare and resolution.

NG: *How does the scriptwriting process work on* Holby City?

SH: On commission, a writer is given a story document which is in essence the five acts of your A, B and C serial element stories which is presented as a page worth of writing from the Story Department. For example, A story– today is Malick's story: he really wants to impress Hanssen on this day he has been put in charge of Keller Ward. It kind of says what should happen. More or less. It gives you the story. And ditto for the B story. B story could be Chrissie's story on AAU and she wants

X but ends up learning Y; C story is Frieda perhaps, whose journey is also similarly charted out in essence. This is what happens to her today. It gives you that story in skeleton, which obviously you really pad out and make your own, not least by creating your own original guest stories to weave in to help drive and illuminate and enrich the serial.

NG: *How are the guest stories developed?*

SH: In the week before commission writers work up with the script editors some guest stories. And that gets signed off prior to commission by the series producer and the senior producer, in terms of whether it's fresh and distinctive enough or whether we've had quite a lot of similar type of stories recently, to decide yes or no. Once that has been signed off, then they can begin.

NG: *What's the time scale from script commission?*

SH: You have your commission conference and then writers go off and do a detailed scene-by-scene. They do up to two scene-by-scenes because it is very important to get that scene-by-scene working. It is a false economy otherwise, given *Holby* is so complex. You want to get those stories down working in the scene-by-scene, with the aim of getting the writer writing within three weeks from that commission. Then they've got two weeks to do their first draft, then I think about ten days to do the second draft and another week for the third.

NG: *Watching* Holby *I noticed that almost all the action takes place on internal sets?*

SH: We very rarely go outside the world. Very occasionally the story department come up with an idea for a story that goes outside of that world. We then get it in the budget; for example, this season, in an episode which I produced, we went out on location to a bridal shop for one of the scenes because it was important to the character's story and dilemma. But by and large you don't. That's another key difference from the *Casualty* format.

NG: *How is the serial element developed?*

SH: What happens is we have story conferences. The whole editorial team plus our core writers will go and sit round a table, go off in groups and come up with a serial long-term story for all our characters.

We need year-long arcs for all of them. Although a year-long arc is 52 episodes you also have to come up with the shorter arcs for them. Although we block in two episodes for development and production purposes, to storyline overall we chop the year-long 52 episode series schedule into mini-series, 14 episodes in each: 1–14, 15–28, 29–42, etc. So at story conferences you work out their arcs for each mini-series, in themselves self-contained. The story department then goes off with a mass of ideas material and they generate those stories into document form, the serial documents I mentioned before that the writers commission off, and they do it bringing in the core writers to storyline with them.

NG: *How big is that team of core writers?*

SH: There are about 20 writers on the writers' list of which ten of them you would call core. Writers go off and do other things. Writers can be hard to hang on to. Some come through the BBC's Writers' Academy and I give out a lot of straight commissions. This year there have been at least 14 new writers on the show.

NG: *Some writers have a fear about the medical aspect of the show. What is your advice to them?*

SH: It is a matter of embracing it. We have consultants in all the disciplines and all of them are good at understanding we need the medicine to service the story. Basically, we have our researchers, who are all great and are all story-minded. As a writer, you are allotted your own researcher who does it all for you. You know Ric is general surgical; you know Jack is cardio-thoracic, so you know the medical area that you want for your guest and their meds and surgeries fall into. Now the researcher may get the most abstract of briefs from the writer. You can brief your researcher very vaguely but you must know what you want it to do in story terms. For example, I want my guest to come in thinking it is an elective and standard procedure but I want something uncovered and underlying that's huge. I want that underlying thing to be something general surgical that brings Ric in. I want Malick to make a mistake. I want it to really go tits up. I want the outcome to be really life-changing for my patient to service this guest story. You can ask the researcher to go out and get something accordingly. From the consultants they get a very detailed medical journey, you know, which they, the researchers, translate into very detailed documents.

NG: *The medicine on the show has to be accurate and make sense. Can that impinge on the storytelling?*

SH: You've got to keep in your mind the logic. Sometimes you can read a script and I can tell they've been given all the medical information by the way they are playing it out but, for example, you suddenly find yourself asking: Wouldn't they have told the patient by this stage what the care plan is? Or you'd question why the patient is still on the ward. Sudden holes in the logic can suddenly appear that it's down to you, the editor and the writer, to think through together. A writer may write that they have a patient who has been in an accident who has been sent up for surgery but suddenly they can't find her notes. However, logic dictates the missing notes would have been picked up in casualty and so it would not be a bombshell in Holby because they would have been told by Charlie Fairhead and co. in that other part of the hospital! It is all about using your common sense. Have the logic in your head.

NG: *What happens when a writer struggles?*

SH: Sometimes, regrettably – and thankfully it doesn't happen that often – we do have to rewrite. There's no getting away from it. It is tough. It is not that they are not good but it is a tall order to write top-notch *Holby City* under tight deadlines. Or you may as a writer regardless of your proven ability not engage with or have the indefinable chemistry and knack with the particular tone, format and characters of this very particular show. Sometimes we have to rewrite: a job which is always given to one of our core writers.

NG: *Do writers have to be fans of* Holby *or at least have done their homework?*

SH: They have to love it. That's the difference in the writing. That's when the characters just sing off the page. When they just love the world and they love the relationships and they have that fun with it and you feel the joy. That's the difference.

Key advice

▶ When writing a spec script for a continuing drama, make sure you have watched as many previous episodes as possible.
▶ You don't have to be a rabid fan, but you should have a feel for the characters and the tone.
▶ All the major UK continuing dramas are different – try to find out as much as you can about the way they are run and the people who head them up.

The broadcasters

In this chapter you will learn:
- *about the main broadcasters in the UK and the range of dramas commissioned or bought by each.*

The broadcasters are the organizations that commission, buy and transmit television programmes. What appears on screen acts as a standard-bearer for that broadcaster and your script must, as a minimum, match the quality that that broadcaster wants to showcase. Broadcasters have different identities, tastes and requirements with regard to television drama.

Let us look at the major UK broadcasters and how they work.

The BBC

The BBC is the biggest producer of drama in the world. Through television, radio and the Internet, the BBC makes approximately 1,000 hours of new, original drama every year and has a back catalogue that is the envy of every other producer/broadcaster in the world. There are a number of channels, each of which has a distinct 'personality', both generally and in terms of its drama output.

BBC1

> **Recent or on-going output:** *Call the Midwife, Casualty, Criminal Justice, Death in Paradise, Doctor Who, EastEnders, Inside Men, Luther, Prisoners' Wives, Sherlock, Wallander, Waterloo Road*

In terms of BBC1 series, there are effectively three time slots available for drama:

▶ Weekdays 9 p.m.–10 p.m.
▶ Saturday evening 7 p.m.–8 p.m.
▶ Weekend/Weekday 8.30 p.m.–10 p.m.

Although BBC1 has gained success with pre-watershed dramas like *Call the Midwife*, *Doctor Who* and *Waterloo Road*, there is a drive to uncover the next returnable series and serials in the nine o'clock slot. The BBC is open to all types of genres for its flagship channel because it understands it needs to provide a broad range of different dramas in a primetime slot. In the current economic cycle the BBC will commission more than 20 series at nine o'clock, including recommissioned shows.

Serials can range from two to six parts, with episodes either 60 or 90 minutes in length. These tend to be stories with a powerful impact like *Occupation* or *Small Island*. These shows may even be stripped over a week like *Five Daughters*.

Single films are self-contained one-off shows up to 90 minutes in length. They can be family entertainment like *The Gruffalo* or real-life stories like *A Short Stay in Switzerland*.

BBC Daytime is commissioned by controller Liam Keelan. In addition to the continuing drama *Doctors*, Keelan hopes to commission 'one big drama per quarter'. Shows have included *Land Girls* and *The Indian Doctor*.

Ben Stephenson, BBC Controller of Drama

'BBC1 drama offers audiences the highest-quality mainstream shows, but it should also take risks with what mainstream drama can be. It should absolutely have the very best in show of all types of drama; singles, serials, series, soap operas, modern and period. Mainstream drama on BBC1 is all about offering audiences drama that moves them in a fundamental way, whether this is through thrills, emotion or humour. BBC1 is ultimately about connecting to people.'

BBC2

> **Recent or on-going output:** *Desperate Romantics*, *Eric and Ernie*,
> *Exile*, *The Shadow Line*, *Night Watch*, *Page Eight*, *United*, *The Hour*,
> *White Heat*

BBC2 is the home of bold and strongly authored serials and single films. Individual episodes can be 60 or 90 minutes long and are mainly geared to the nine o'clock slot.

Ben Stephenson, BBC Controller of Drama
'In 2011 BBC2 had a massive injection of cash, doubling the budget. I wanted to restore the reputation of what BBC2 can do and I was thrilled that we took our average audience from 1.9 to 2.9 million. I think we found a tone and an ambition that really connected to the audience and also to writers, directors and actors. BBC2 drama is all about bringing an alternative point of view to the screen – this may be about the way a story is told, or about the type of story we tell. I found that the minute we said we wanted drama on BBC2 we had things arrive we would never have had otherwise, so it actually encouraged and broadened the range of drama the writers were writing.'

BBC3

> **Recent or on-going output:** *Being Human*, *The Fades*

BBC3 is mainly skewed to a young 16–34 audience and so the drama series on this channel need to be authentic and distinctive and laced with humour. The current position is that BBC3 can commission only one or two series a year.

Ben Stephenson, BBC Controller of Drama
'BBC3 is deliberately there to cater for the audience that the other channels might not cater for. Due to the licence fee settlement, we will be decreasing the amount of drama on BBC3 to probably one or two dramas a year. Obviously shows such as *Being Human*, *Lip Service* and *The Fades* demonstrate what BBC3 is there to do, which is to bring a broad audience to the subject matter in a way that engages a young audience.'

All writers are equal

'All good writers are equal. It is not about being a name. *Prisoners' Wives* was written by Julie Geary who had never had her own series before and we commissioned *Death in Paradise* by Robert Thorogood who had never written anything ever. I just read those scripts and I really liked them.'

It is all about the script

'I suspect some producers may feel that a project will be quicker to screen with a so-called A-list writer, but I just want good scripts. If I am to make a decision between a brilliant script by an unknown Joe Bloggs and a not-so-good one by someone really famous, I'd be mad to go with the not-so-good one. For me, it's all about making really good TV and a responsibility to work with the best writers in the country whether they are incredibly established or incredibly new, and regardless of fame. So ultimately what will get you a quick commission? A brilliant script.'

The audience rules

'I'm not particularly concerned about critics. For me it is about audiences. If no one was watching any of our dramas, then that would be a problem. For each show we know we have to deliver in a different way. *Occupation*, which we did three years ago, just as an example, got three and a half million on BBC1, which was absolutely fine. However, if the second series of a populist drama got 3 million that would be less good."

Hits and failures

'You can't insure against failure. If you do you won't ever create a hit because you'll be so terrified of anything that feels different that you'll never commission anything that might connect in a challenging and fresh way. Ultimately, hits are shows that audiences love for their distinctiveness and originality. In retrospect, people think hits are obvious. People think *Call the Midwife* and *Sherlock* were obvious hits. I assure you they were not. Some things are clearly bigger risks than others, but in their own mainstream way both these dramas were big risks for a variety of reasons. So, if you're scared of failure, don't commission these shows, but also don't ever expect to have a hit.'

On commissioning
'The questions to ask are: firstly, is it an idea that you feel the audience will engage with? No one turns on the television thinking, 'I've no idea what this is about but I hope it's good.' You turn it on because you think that the idea is appealing. So you have to ask yourself: Is it an interesting idea? Is it fresh, is it distinctive? Secondly, you have to ask yourself the question: Is the script a complete iteration of its idea? Thirdly, do the team who are working on it, by which I mean the writer and the production team, have a completely clear vision of the show that they are making? Fourthly, do they have an unerring commitment to and passion for the show? Would they lie down in front of a train to make it? If every answer to one of those is yes, then you should make it.'

ITV

Recent or on-going output: *Downton Abbey*, *Injustice*, *Love Life*, *Midsomer Murders*, *Scott & Bailey*, *Titanic*, *Whitechapel*

ITV is the UK's longest-serving commercial broadcaster. Drama is the cornerstone of the schedule, combining long-serving continuing dramas *Coronation Street* and *Emmerdale* with original post-watershed drama playing out at nine o'clock three or four times a week throughout the year. ITV's flagship channel, ITV1, broadcasts the vast majority of the dramas, though ITV2 occasionally broadcasts original British drama such as *Diary of a Call Girl*, *Trinity* and *The Witches*.

ITV seeks to make as many of its own shows as possible via its independent production arm, ITV Studios, but it also commissions shows from other independent production companies.

Victoria Fea is a commissioning executive for ITV. In a 19-year career she has worked as a script editor, producer and executive producer including a spell as Creative Director at BBC Drama Production.

Victoria Fea, ITV Drama Commissioning Executive, on...

Sample scripts

'An idea isn't enough. I can have a good idea but I'm not a writer. Anyone can write an idea. Anyone can have a paragraph or half a page that they have come up with. The thing I always say to new writers in particular is that you have got to have a sample that is your voice. It needs to be at least 60 minutes and in an ideal world it has to be 90 minutes. You have got be able to write and structure and storyline a film-length narrative because that is going to be your calling card because whoever hires you, even if it's as an episodic writer on another show or long-runner, if they can't hear your voice in the first place they can't tell. Certainly, I can't tell what I think about a writer until I've read something that is theirs, completely theirs, not an episode of *Casualty* or an episode of *Holby*; I mean something they've written from the heart. When someone submits an idea and it is a writer that I don't actually know or I haven't worked with or read before, I will say I need a sample. I don't mind whatever they've written on – if I don't have first-hand experience of them, then I need to read a script that is not a series.'

Development

'We do a lot of development here. It very rarely starts with a script on a desk – it is usually an idea in a room with a producer and the writer may or may not be in that room, but basically it starts with an idea. It is very, very occasionally that a script drops on the desk that has been developed elsewhere, that someone has done off their own back, but usually it is just the normal development process. I have an assistant who is a reader who deals with general submissions and if a script comes in that we don't really know why it has come in or where it has come from, and we don't have a relationship with that person, I will ask the reader to read it because it is less likely that it would be something we would want to do.'

Preferred writers

'We're always saying to producers: we don't expect you to give the A-listers all the time. We're waiting for them anyway. They're on our slate. It's just they are not free. If they are free, they are doing something for us. The only criteria we have is that the writer who originates a brand-new idea for us is capable of creating something that is commercial, that's mainstream, popular telly. The only thing we need here is an audience. We don't care whether the writer has written for television before. One of our frontrunner projects as I speak, although we're not greenlit, is by a writer who has written a handful of plays but has never written for TV. So we don't really mind about experience. The truth is you're more likely be able to hit a sweet spot with ITV if you are an experienced mainstream writer. It is very rare to get straight off the blocks with a writer and have all those tools at your disposal to be able to create something from scratch that will speak to the ITV audience and be a hit. That is quite rare to do that without experience. It is easier to cut your teeth on things that don't have that commercial pressure.'

What ITV wants

'We are pretty loud and clear about what we want all the time, actually. We say it at every road show and we say it at every general meeting with an indie. A few times a year we go round the big agencies and we talk with the writers' agents. ITV is a commercial channel. We need an audience. We're not ashamed of that. That's how all the channels operate in the States. None of us believe you leave quality at the door in order to get an audience because that would be a depressing thought. So it is a very clear proposition at ITV. It is very clear what we need to achieve. The stakes are very high. It is less clear at the BBC what they have to achieve. They have to have something for everybody. They have to be pluralist because we all pay for it. At ITV we need an audience. It is very clear what we need to do at this channel. It is very scary. The stakes are so high and it is pretty black and white. It is very easy to say no because if something is not naturally a commercial, mainstream idea we can't do it.'

ITV being the crime channel
'We're always saying we don't want to be the crime channel. That's why we have *Downton Abbey*. That's why we made *Marchlands*. That's why we make five singles a year. We're constantly saying we really don't want to be the crime channel. We have to deliver crime because that's what our audience responds to but we have had a moratorium on detectives for months now. That's why *Downton* was so brilliant for the channel. In one hit it suddenly declared we're not just crime!'

Pitching to ITV
'People sometimes email us a one-liner or a paragraph, or in a general meeting people will pitch us things – we look at verbal pitches. They'll send us a page or two pages. Sometimes someone will send me a sample and say 'This writer's brilliant. Do you agree?' and I'll say 'Yes, I love that sample – it's fantastic' and please encourage them if they've got that natural ITV voice. I will probably also inquire about their experience because if I read a sample that's brilliant and that person has written a couple of episodes for a couple of series, they have kind of cut their teeth on the process of what it is like to write because in television it is a process, and then I'll be really excited. Basically, we'll respond to an idea and we'll kill it straight dead or we'll encourage it to bits.'

Calculated risks
'We take calculated risks. It depends on the taste of the Director of Television. Peter Fincham has got very sound mainstream tastes but he likes to take creative risks. So you can tell with the *Marchlands* format that is an accessible idea because it's about a family across decades. There is a slight genre thread but it is about the death of a child so that is going to hook in our

audience. The families everyone can relate to that – there's a kind of accessibility to it. There was a spookiness to it and actually, was it all just in their heads? There actually wasn't a ghost in *Marchlands* but it felt different enough. It sort of stood out. So that was a really clever calculated risk. There was a way in for our audience but at the same time we were pushing them towards something unexpected for the channel. So that's what you can do on ITV – you can do calculated risks every now and again. You have to be confident to take risks. You have to be in a place where things are going OK.'

Pushing ITV's parameters
'It is far better for the writers and indies to push us and for us to pull them back because wouldn't it be boring if everyone self-edited all the time? You're never going to get breakthrough surprise shows like that. When *Downton Abbey* came here there was a moratorium on period drama. Then Gareth Neame said: "What about Julian Fellowes writing the series of *Gosford Park*?" ITV went: "OK we'll just have a look at that." So you want people to ignore you quite a lot of the time but then trust you when you say: "That was really brave but actually it just isn't going to get an audience." That hopefully sets up a relationship whereby you are encouraging people to follow their passions and go for their instincts and allow writers to write what they want to write while you act as the editor.'

Original period drama
'A BBC period show is usually, in the eyes of the audience anyway, literary and more often than not a literary classic and an adaptation. Both Laura Mackie and Sally Haynes who commissioned *Downton Abbey* were very much of the view that ITV don't do remakes and ITV don't do adaptations. Now ITV does *original* period writing. They wouldn't have done *Upstairs, Downstairs* – it was a remake. We do *Downton Abbey* because it is original writing and it's very authored.

Year-round commissioning
'Obviously we're commissioning for very specific slots, so we might commission all year round but we know what we're aiming for.

We don't commission willy-nilly. You commission for a slot and you commission for a season. So in November we commissioned a raft of things for next autumn.'

Greenlighting a show

'What we're pretty strict about is, we won't greenlight a series idea without two scripts. We'll commission a serial quite often on Episode 1, but a series idea we will greenlight after we've read Episode 1 and 2 and the storylines, but there's rarely enough time to develop all the scripts before you shoot.'

Recommissioning

'These days the magic number is five. If something is consolidating – I mean not just the overnights but the catch-up as well at well over 5 million – it's a bit of a no-brainer. Even then you usually wait until the end of the run. It has to be massive for us to recommission during the run. Why would we? If you wait, you can get the research and look at all the consolidated figures – sometimes they go up 1 million, 1.5 million with catch-up. You can get some focus group stuff done. Obviously, things like that are really valuable when things are sort of on the cusp. We want to discuss it. We don't actually leave people hanging on for very long.'

The first episode

'The first episode has to declare what the series is going to be because you can't put subtitles saying: "Stay with us – this is going to happen in Series 3." The audience only has the first episode to judge. Really, they've only got the first ten minutes!'

Audience reaction

'The brutal reality is that the audience decides very quickly. They decide in the first 15 minutes of Episode 1 of a brand-new series and it's very unusual to claw back from that. It's quite difficult to decide if something hasn't hit the sweet spot in its first run – are you really going to risk taking it back and watch the figures go down even more in a second series?'

What a good ITV script needs

'Good story, character and dialogue. They're the three things to worry about. Here at ITV it has to be entertaining and that means it grips the audience, it invites them in, it starts a story that they find accessible, that they understand but which also might surprise them and reward them. Our pieces have got to be entertaining. Entertaining means it can make you cry and it can make you laugh, and it could involve murder and detection and revolution but in the end it has got to be entertaining. It has got to be a good journey to go on for our audience.'

Other channels' content

'I think everyone is conscious of what the opposition is doing. Each channel has a different role to play and a different role for the audience. Audiences come to different channels with different expectations, which is why you can do things on ITV that you couldn't do on BBC1. You couldn't have made *Appropriate Adult* on BBC1. The BBC could not have been seen to make a drama about Fred West, but we felt it was a story that demanded to be told and done sensibly and was the absolutely right thing to do for our audience, and it was. We wouldn't have done an adaptation of *South Riding*. We wouldn't do *Great Expectations*. So there are different expectations from the audience and the only difference is that ITV is the only channel that has to get a mainstream audience. The BBC partly has to do that but it also has to do lots of other things.'

The effects of a hit

'*Sherlock* on BBC1 and *Downton Abbey* on ITV have both had a very positive effect on the drama industry. As everyone has realized that you don't have to follow convention; you don't have to tick certain boxes. You can surprise people; you can still take creative risks and have a big hit. I think a lot of people; have found it quite refreshing and found it inspiring that the goal posts have moved.'

ITV2

'ITV2 is also a mainstream channel so its shows need to have a broad appeal but it is younger-skewing. It's inclusive, it's entertaining, it's warm and it's inviting. It's not too cool for school.

It doesn't say: grown-ups are not allowed here. It is just a different version of the main channel, which is why we can't do things that clash with the main channel. ITV2 has to complement the main channel but it is the same DNA in many ways.'

Channel 4

Recent or on-going output: Serials – *The Promise*, *Top Boy*, *This Is England*; Series (often comedy-drama) – *Shameless*, *Fresh Meat* (both C4), *Misfits*, *Skins* (both E4)

Channel 4 is a publisher-broadcaster, which means that they don't make programmes themselves. All of their commissioned content is made by the independent sector. In terms of drama, Channel 4 currently commissions single films (one or two per year), serials (two or three per year in two, three, four or five parts) and series, while its sister channel, E4, concentrates on series.

Ben Stoll, Head of Development at Channel 4 Drama, on...

Drama series
'Series tend to be comedy-drama; they tend to be at the funnier end of the spectrum: *Shameless* and *Fresh Meat* on Channel 4; and these are broad brushstrokes because obviously those shows do deal with darker storylines as well. On E4 *Skins* and *Misfits* tend to skew younger. Again, there is a lot of room for comedy even if they do deal with some dark material, too.'

Singles and serials
'When it comes to the singles and serials, the singles often have something serious to say about the world. We don't want to beat the audience over the head with an issue. We don't want to be didactic but we do want to ask awkward and interesting questions.'

Distinctive drama

'One of our challenges and one of our ambitions is to stay fresh and surprising. We hope that we commission ideas and scripts that perhaps wouldn't get commissioned elsewhere, for example *Top Boy* and *This Is England*. We think this is a natural home for projects like that. We're after what we hope and believe to be the best projects.'

The difference between drama on C4 and E4

'E4 certainly skews younger and there is certain flexibility in the playing around with genre. Take *Misfits*, which sits well on E4 but perhaps wouldn't sit so well on Channel 4. These are self-imposed boundaries and they are part of our rules. There has got be an element of instinct and examination at what is really at the heart of a show. *Fresh Meat* plays on Channel 4. It could be argued because it has a core cast of younger characters that it should sit on E4, but it felt like it was dealing with issues in a grown-up world, in the real world.

The commissioning process

'That's an on-going thing. Those are on-going conversations we have every day with independents and writers. I guess one of the most important things for us is to be talking to producers all the time and, of course, our priorities will shift and change according to the shows that get greenlit. Not massively and radically but there are always nudges in one direction or another.'

What C4 looks for

'Fundamentally we're looking for the best material. There are a hundred different ways of going about that. People will pitch us ideas all the time or we might have a sense that we are interested in a territory and we will talk to people. We don't know what it could be but it is a two-way conversation.'

Preferred indies

'We work with bigger independents who make programmes for all the major broadcasters and we also work with much smaller and newer independents who are just finding their drama voice, their drama feet. It is always project-dependent. It's not about the company as much as the project.'

Commissioning writers

'We commission a writer through an independent. We actually contract the company, who will in turn contract the writer. That's how the structure works. But yes, we're in touch with writers all the time. Ultimately, the writer's most important relationship isn't with us; it will be with the producer. It will be down to them and who they want to work with.'

All writers are equal

'It's absolutely project-dependent. We work with new writers on *Skins* and we work with very experienced writers like Peter Flannery, Peter Kominsky (*The Promise*) and Ronan Bennett (*Top Boy*). So we absolutely have a range and a spectrum that we cannot afford to miss out on and we would not want to limit ourselves. It is all about the best material. We don't want to rule anything out.'

Hollyoaks

'It is a brilliant and massively important show for us. It has been consistently popular and successful for a very long time. It does something quite unique, actually. It fits with everything else. It sits as our only home-grown pre-watershed drama soap. It's fantastic.'

What's *not* Channel 4

'Broadly speaking, and these are general rules, we aren't perhaps looking for straightforward genre pieces, medical, legal, cop shows. Those territories are very well catered for elsewhere. I suppose we always look for a surprising spin, a surprising take, a surprising angle on things. Again, apart from *Hollyoaks*, our home-grown drama is always post-watershed that suggests a certain attitude and tone.'

Channel 4 boundaries

'We're not looking for swearing for the sake of it. The sorts of stories you tell have got to be part of the DNA of the show. We're not out to shock for shock's sake.'

Reading scripts

'I don't look at a script and try and catch it out. What I'm looking for is to be surprised, entertained, amused. I'm looking for positives. I'm looking to turn the pages. I want to know what is going to happen in the end. These are all the sort of obvious things which are hard to achieve for any writer.'

Channel 4 drama success

'There are different kinds of success. Of course, you have to take viewing figures into account because ultimately we are here to serve an audience. There's critical success. We try to take everything into account and also reputations. We think some projects deserve their place on screen because we believe passionately that there's a voice that should be heard whether it gets massive numbers or not. We have a broad set of criteria.'

Channel 4's public service obligations

'It can be a challenge but that's what makes this place unique and exciting. We do get opportunities to commission shows and films that may not have the commercial success in the traditional sense. They may not get numbers. That is not necessarily a reason not to commission them. For example, *Random*, a film we did last year, is currently shortlisted for an RTS Award in the Single Drama category. It was a great film. A really interesting, moving, provocative film and we don't regret commissioning that for a minute.'

The British point of view

'The stories we commission, whether they are set here or not, reflect back on this country. So *The Promise*, for example, is set in Palestine/Israel but is told from a British point of view. Of course, our great acquisitions team also buy in mainly American shows like *Homeland*. And yet we do have a clear sense of purpose in that respect. When we look at a show we're looking at it for a domestic audience.'

Single films

'Singles tend to ask those more difficult questions about live issues and the serials do all sorts of things.'

Advice to writers

'Keep going if you believe that is what you want to do. Learn as much as you can. Immerse yourself in what you do, in your craft. Watch television. Read scripts if you can get hold of them. See how other people do it. See what works; see what doesn't work. You need to get an agent. You need to meet producers. I will say, if TV is really the medium you want to write for, immerse yourself in it, watch it, read scripts if you can get hold of them, study it but not in an academic way. Get on the inside of it and ask yourself questions about what you like, what you don't like, why you like something, why you think it works, why you're having that emotional response and look at the way the story is told. The point is about good writing that there is something a little bit magical about it and you can't analyse that. You can look at structure. You can look at how scenes are constructed and how character journeys are delineated but there's always that X factor that none of us quite understands and that is the writer's take on the world.'

Initiatives for new writers

'We run two schemes for new writers – *Coming Up*, now in its eleventh year, where selected writers are guaranteed a broadcast commission, and 4Screenwriting, where selected writers experience the development process. We've had success with both.'

Sky

Recent or on-going output: Sky1HD – *Going Postal, Little Crackers, Mad Dogs, The Runaway, Sinbad, Strike Back, Thorne, Treasure Island*; Sky Atlantic – *Falcon, Hit and Miss;* Sky Living – *Bedlam*; Sky Arts – *Playhouse Presents*

Sky Television currently has five channels for which it commissions original UK drama: Sky1HD, Sky Atlantic, Sky Living, Sky Arts and Sky Movies. Sky1 has a commitment to original UK drama production but those shows have to stand up to the best of the American imports. Sky Atlantic looks for iconic drama that stands out among its new American dramas. Sky Living is a station of what is described as fresh and innovative programming. Sky Arts looks for well-scripted, high-end drama. Sky Movies wants single features that are big, family brands. In this respect, known adaptations from books is a preference.

Essentially, Sky drama aims to be fun and entertaining, but the ambition is to be big and broad in ambition. There is a desire to produce longer runs that range between four and 13 episodes and to have an outward look that gives the drama an almost transatlantic feel in terms of production values. British content has to sit comfortably among the American imports.

Sky, however, does not have in-house production. Like Channel 4, it is currently a publisher-broadcaster, which means all submissions must come via an independent production company. Co-productions, particularly international co-productions, are very important because Sky wants as much money as possible on screen so that the original content can compete visually with big-budget American imports.

Key advice

▶ Try to watch as much British TV drama as you and across the full range of broadcasters.
▶ Try to develop an idea of the characteristic range and tone of the dramas commissioned by individual broadcasters and where your particular voice might fit best.
▶ Remember, however: originality is the key value that all broadcasters are looking for.

18

TV scriptwriting in the United States

In this chapter you will learn:
- **how the US scriptwriting industry differs from its counterpart in the UK**
- **the main US broadcasters**
- **the differences in the drama output of the network and cable broadcasters.**

In the US, in contrast to the UK, agents and studios want to look at not only a writer's original script for a pilot but also a spec script of the show they wish to write for. In the UK the industry prefers to see only original work and then, if they are interested, will ask you to write a trial script for the show. No one is interested in your script for their show.

The US has a different model and a bigger television industry. Industry executives not only want to see your original voice but also whether you understand and can write for their show.

Overview

WRITING A SPEC SCRIPT

If you're going to write a spec script for an existing show with a view to getting a commission, choose a show that interests you. You may already be a fan and that helps. However, given how the staffing season works, it is important to select a show that will return the following year. There is no benefit to writing a spec script of a show that has been cancelled or come to the end of its life.

A TV series spec script is a particular document that shows off your writing talent as to whether people think you can write for that show. Choose your show and not only watch as many episodes as you can but *study* it. Look at the structure, the character dynamics, the tone. You have to capture the voice of the show.

As an example, let us look at the hit TV show *Bones*, which, in 2012, started its seventh season.

Bones, created by Hart Hanson

Bones is a classic 'whodunit?'. Each episode is based around a murder and our heroes' successful pursuit and apprehension of the murderer.

The show opens with **'The Find'**, which invariably involves the discovery of a body by civilians. This involves the audience being enticed to look at something unpleasant but which piques their interest.

This opening sequence rarely involves the two leads. There is a practical reason for this – namely, it gives the two main stars (Emily Deschanel and David Borenaz) a pause in the punishing production schedule since one or both are involved in virtually every other scene in the script.

There are other key components that feature in every episode – for example, Brennan's **'Big Moment'**, which is when she uncovers the final clue that leads to the murderer. Booth, too, has his own 'big moment', which is an intuition about someone or something that, despite the lack of concrete evidence, turns out to be true.

Then there is the moment when at least one of our heroes is in the room with the killer and his/her identity is revealed and we learn the motive. The *Bones* staff call this **'The Download'** and it should be delivered in the most economical way possible. Long *Poirot*-style summing-up has no place here.

It is important that the murderer must always have a character-driven reason why they killed the person. It is also part of *Bones'* DNA that the murderer should never be a surprise. It will always be a character the audience has met in the first half of the episode.

The other element that seems to appear in every episode is when Brennan will reveal or talk about something personal to Booth (or another character). This is rather comically described by the staff as the **'Glug, Glug, Whoopee Moment'**!

Each show has its own way of doing things on screen, its own formula which, hopefully, won't be formulaic in an obvious way. It will be a formula that works and goes unnoticed by the audience. The moment the audience is on to it, the show becomes predictable and less of an enjoyable experience.

With any existing show, make sure your spec script features a story that is about and profoundly affects the main characters. Make the story personal to your main character and not just anybody, but at the same time the emotional integrity has to strike a universal chord. Do not introduce a new character and make the story about them – that's what your original spec script is for. You can, however, utilize an underserved existing character and out them into the spotlight. Indeed, the screenwriter Jane Espenson has almost specialized in making support characters shine.

SCRIPT READERS

In the US script readers at agents, management companies and studios have a simple three-category marking system. A script will be deemed either RECOMMEND, CONSIDER or PASS:

RECOMMEND This is the highest assessment level and the script reader recommends the script should be looked at people higher up the chain, who in turn will make an judgement as to whether it gets higher still. A 'recommend' usually leads to a meeting (see below).

CONSIDER This is where the reader believes the script has potential but not sure whether it is ready. The script will probably be looked at by other readers and assessed.

PASS This is what 95 per cent of all scripts in Hollywood receive. It is an outright rejection, usually accompanied by a benign stock covering letter.

In certain circumstances the 'pass' may be given not because the script is badly written but because it is just not suitable for that particular company. The same script may be deemed suitable somewhere else.

Remember, everything is television is subjective and nobody knows of certainties.

THE MEETING

If you do get a meeting with a show, you should arrive armed with specific ideas – preferably not re-treads of previously aired episodes – and an understanding of the show – about what works and what doesn't – although your spec script should already have helped you there.

US STAFFING

Most US television drama series are written by staff writers, although there are occasional single freelance opportunities. A successful freelance written episode may lead to a staff position the following season. Your breakthrough goal, of course, is get on a writing staff of one of the commissioned series. This is where your excellently scripted original spec leads the way and, if it is an existing series, your show spec script.

THE WRITERS' ROOM

Ideally, you want a writers' room to be a place where each member of the writing staff has a deep investment in the momentum and voice of the series. Like any workplace, a TV writers' room can be run in a myriad of different ways, mainly coloured by the showrunner, who, in most cases, is the original creator of the show. It can be a pleasant, rewarding experience or an unpleasant, unsatisfying one.

In general terms, US network TV series can run up to 24 episodes a season while cable networks have shorter runs of up to 13 episodes – and the season is king. A writer not only writes scripts but will have to demonstrate the ability to solve story problems quickly, preferably with an original take.

The writers' room will break stories, by character, by episode, by multi-episode and by series collectively. Outlines can be written (which can vary in length from show to show – for example, *Nip/Tuck* had 7 to 10-page outlines). One of the writers will be assigned to write an episode. On delivery of the first draft, the writers' room then tears it apart, ostensibly to make it better. Further drafts may follow and ultimately the showrunner can rewrite the episode and, on most shows, invariably does.

US broadcasters

THE NETWORKS

In the US there are five major television networks – often referred to collectively as 'the Networks' – which commission and make original drama. The shows are often created with an independent production company who license shows to broadcasters. There may be other co-production partners to help finance and make the show happen.

The five major television networks are: ABC, CBS, NBC, Fox and The CW. All five networks are unashamedly commercial in nature and it is all about advertising revenue, which is dictated by the viewing public. People have to watch in big numbers for the networks to continue to commit their vast investment.

Advertisers are a powerful force in the US television landscape and there have been rare occasions when advertisers have boycotted or withdrawn their ads for particular shows. In many ways most of Network television is standard fare, albeit high-quality, well-made standard fare that attracts millions of viewers. If something works, they stick with it until it fails.

Take CBS, for example, which knows its audiences love cop shows to the extent that successful shows not only earn a spin-off but a whole family of spin-offs. Both CSI and NCIS now both have several spin-off shows. It produces drama series, mini-series and movies for television, as do all the five big networks.

NBC, a natural rival of CBS, has cop/investigative shows as its core, too. Even a seemingly genre show such as *Grimm* in which the world is inhabited by fairy-tale characters is essentially in style and structure a detective show with a murder to solve. That is not to say that this network is not open to other ideas. It is. *Smash*, for example, launched to great acclaim as the *Glee* for grown-ups.

ABC also likes its cop and doc shows as the bedrock of its schedules, but when it has strayed into different dramatic territory it has had a number of remarkable hits including *Desperate Housewives*, *Lost* and *Once Upon a Time*. On its teenage-skewing ABC Family channel, it commissions shows such as *Pretty Little Liars, The Secret Life of the American Teenager* and *Switched at Birth*.

Fox has probably the most diverse range of drama in its schedules and is unashamedly populist in its approach(as are the other networks). There is room for docs and cops in the form of *House* and *Bones* but also more cinematic concepts with shows such as *Fringe* and *Touch*. Fox also has a cable station called FX that allows it to make edgier drama, for example *Rescue Me, Sons of Anarchy* and *American Horror Story*.

The fifth major network is The CW. This has a young demographic with teenagers at its core and the shows reflect that. The main characters tend be young and aspirational.

All five networks make high-budget drama and the money shows in the high production values evident on screen as they compete for the lucrative US audience. However, the power of advertisers does place a constraint on the tone and content. All the shows rarely have content of an overtly sexual nature, excessive swearing or graphic violence. However, both writers and programme-makers know this and work within the parameters. If they don't, none of the networks will look at their show. The networks cannot risk offending advertisers.

The bottom line is shows have to make money through advertising and syndication. Below is a list of leading network shows. For all their formulaic storytelling they are all a success through their use of strong lead characters, an identifiable premise and an assured tone. The list should give an indication of the flavour of each channel:

ABC *Alias, Body of Proof, Boston Legal, Brothers & Sisters, Castle, Desperate Housewives, Grey's Anatomy, Lost, Missing, Once Upon a Time, Pan Am, The Practice, Rookie Blue, Scandal*

CBS *Blue Bloods, CSI: Crime Scene Investigation, CSI: Miami, CSI: New York, The Good Wife, Hawaii Five-O, The Mentalist, NCIS, NCIS: Los Angeles, Unforgettable*
Fox *Bones, Fringe, Glee, House, Touch*
NBC *Burn Notice, Chuck, The Firm, Friday Night Lights, Grimm, Harry's Law, Law & Order, Law & Order: Los Angeles, Law & Order: Special Victims Unit, Smash*
The CW *90210, Gossip Girl, Nikita, Ringer, Supernatural, The Secret Circle, The Vampire Diaries*

A brief guide to US television drama commissioning (Networks)

Pitching season
This takes place in the summer from July and is where ideas that have been developed by individual writers or writing teams with agencies and production companies are brought to the attention of the Networks. This is a kind of feeding frenzy and the Networks suggest what they are looking for, something which is coloured by the number of slots in their schedule they have available. Existing returning series are already bedded in, so all the new shows are battling for what is left.

Writing the pilot season
Out of the pitches around about a fifth will go on to the next stage, which is the writing of the pilot episode script. The target is to deliver the best possible script – no doubt after many drafts – to the Networks by November.

Pilot commissioning season
Once all the pilot scripts have been read and assessed by the Networks, then once again between a fifth and a quarter will be greenlit for production. By the end of January all the pilots have been ordered. All this means is that one episode of your series will get made, though everyone hopes the series will run for at least four seasons of between 88 and 100 episodes (and thus lead to money-making syndication).

Pilot production season

Over the next two months the pilot episodes go into production and are delivered to the Networks. Once they are delivered they are screen-tested before audiences. After that, with possibly some re-editing, the pilots are sent to the top people at the Networks for 'the upfronts'.

The upfronts

This takes place in May and is where the top executives decide which of those pilots they are going to commission for a series. They will simply say yes or no. If it is a no – you have to bite the bullet. If it is a yes, then the options are:

▶ a **full season** of 22–26 episodes. However, usually only the first 13 episodes are committed to; if the show is successful, the rest of the season will be taken up.

▶ a **short order** of 4–6 episodes. This is US conservative commissioning at its best. It is a 'defer and see' policy. If the series is not an instant success, no more episodes will be commissioned.

▶ a **mid-season**. This is when a show is given a later broadcast date (but also a shorter run), usually as a replacement for the inevitable cancelled shows that debut and quickly die.

It is an overtly commercial system and solely depends on 'bums on sofas'. If not enough people tune into the show, the Networks have no scruples about it pulling the show even after only two episodes have been aired.

CABLE

In recent years the subscription-based cable broadcasters that used to be home to syndicated Network shows have made forays into original drama output. This move was led by HBO and following in its wake have been the likes of AMC, Showtime and Starz.

The series and serials produced for cable often have shorter runs (a maximum of 13 episodes). The most significant factor, however, is that the original shows that appear on these channels are very different to the fare that appears on the Networks. Since most are subscription-based, they are not exclusively beholden to advertisers but to the viewers. The approach has been to make drama that is ambitious, bold, innovative and riskier.

HBO has led the way to a large extent. The HBO business model is not dependent on advertisers but viewer subscriptions. HBO shows do not have ad breaks and run, like the BBC, uninterrupted for the full hour. Since, arguably, HBO has a direct contract with the viewer, it can broadcast shows that shown elsewhere might offend advertisers.

HBO dramas – some of which are international co-productions – can be more 'adult' in terms of their use of profanity, violence and scenes of a sexual nature. That is not to say that this 'adult content' is written into the shows for the sake of it. All swearing, sex and violence has to be relevant and important to the story.

All the major networks love cop shows but none of them was ever going to show *The Wire*. Its natural home was HBO, as otherwise the scale and nature of the storytelling would inevitably have been homogenized and made bland. It would certainly not have been *The Wire* as envisaged by creator David Simon.

HBO content has been different as it has been diverse. It has made award-winning dramas that have taken subscribers into the world of the Wild West, Prohibition America and the fantasy world of *Game of Thrones*. They have broadcast adapted novels including *Game of Thrones* and *Mildred Pierce*.

In recent years other cable networks have begun supporting and producing their own original scripted content. They have been equally ambitious in carving out their own distinctive type of drama. AMC has won plaudits for *Mad Men*, *Breaking Bad* and *The Walking Dead* and has also reworked the cult Danish drama *Forbrydelsen* as *The Killing*.

Showtime, which is a subsidiary of CBS, has also made distinctive dramas that would not play on the main CBS network. *Dexter* and *Homeland* have been big successes, as have Showtime's historical dramas *The Borgias* and *The Tudors*.

Below is a list of leading cable shows:

AMC *Breaking Bad, The Killing, Mad Men, Rubicon, The Walking Dead*

HBO *Band of Brothers, Boardwalk Empire, Deadwood, Game of Thrones, Luck, Mildred Pierce, Six Feet Under, True Blood, The Sopranos, The Wire*

Showtime *The Borgias, Dead Like Me, Dexter, Homeland, Shameless, The Tudors*

Starz *Magic City, Spartacus, Torchwood: Miracle Day.*

A brief guide of US television drama commissioning (cable)

The US cable commissioning system is similar to the British system in the sense that commissioning takes place all year round. Furthermore, the seasons are shorter and can be anywhere between six and 13 episodes.

Key advice

▶ The US TV drama industry is both much bigger and tougher than its UK counterpart.

▶ Most scripts are produced in-house by staff writers.

▶ The vast majority of US TV drama output is dominated by the need to pull in advertising, which can lead to a certain blandness.

▶ On the other hand, because of the competition for viewers (and hence advertisers), production values are usually very high.

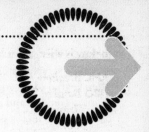

Taking it further

Scriptwriting courses

There are many and varied scriptwriting courses available to writers, from one-day workshops about a particular aspect of scriptwriting to a university four-year Master's degree. As with all courses, research thoroughly what it is the right one for you and also consider the cost. In the UK universities can now charge up to £9,000 per year while in the US the equivalent courses can cost almost $50,000 in tuition fees for the complete course.

Below is a list of some of the UK universities that offer undergraduate and/or postgraduate courses in screenwriting. Most courses are offered as part-time or full-time and the course duration varies as a result.

> Bournemouth University (www.bournemouth.ac.uk)
> City University, London (www.city.ac.uk)
> De Montfort University, Leicester (www.dmu.ac.uk)
> Napier University, Edinburgh (www.courses.napier.ac.uk)
> Goldsmiths, University of London (www.goldsmiths.ac.uk)
> John Moores University, Liverpool (www.ljmu.ac.uk)
> London College of Communication (www.lcc.arts.ac.uk)
> London Film School (www.lfs.org.uk)
> London School of Film, Media & Performance (www.lsfmp.ac.uk)
> National Film and Television School, Beaconsfield (www.nfts.ac.uk)
> Newport Film School (www.amd.newport.ac.uk)
> Sheffield Hallam University (www.shu.ac.uk)
> Southampton University (www.solent.ac.uk)
> University of Bolton (www.bolton.ac.uk)
> University of Central Lancashire, Preston (www.uclan.ac.uk)
> University of East Anglia (www.uea.ac.uk)
> University of Sunderland (www.sunderland.ac.uk)
> University of the West of Scotland, Ayr (www.uws.ac.uk)

In the US there are a number of university courses that range from specialist screenwriting programmes to Master's degrees. These are often geared to getting writers working in the industry, although this is not automatic and there are no guarantees. However, there have been notable successes – for example, the University of Southern California (USC) boasts Shonda Rhymes, who created *Grey's Anatomy*, and Josh Schwartz, who created *Chuck*.

Getting on these courses is a competitive business because each year the numbers are limited, as they are for all university courses. There are many courses run by various universities and organizations throughout North America but, arguably, the five leading institutions are:

American Film Institute (AFI), Los Angeles (www.afi.com)
Colombia University, New York (www.columbia.edu)
New York University (NYU) (www.nyu.edu)
University of California (UCLA) (www.tft.ucla.edu)
University of Southern California (USC) School of Cinematic Arts,
    Los Angeles (www.cinema.usc.edu)

These five institutions are in the two major cities where the television industry is based and they draw thousands of applicants each year.

Do check the nature of the course and the tutors involved and, more importantly, what and who the graduate success stories are. While there may be benefits to undertaking such a course, there can be no guarantees and you should also realize that university is not the only way into the business.

Various individuals and organizations run other short courses, some of which are residential. Again the fees can be variable – from quite competitive and open to most pockets to the four-figure range. Do your research, particularly concerning the tutor(s), and try and speak to others who have been on the course.

Sources for scripts

There are a number of websites that allow you to download scripts either for free or for a fee. Be aware that some websites offer transcripts of scripts which, as a general rule, are not helpful. If you can't get a shooting script version, then a writer's earlier draft is equally worth reading. Here is a list of websites where you can download TV scripts:

```
www.bbcwritersroom.co.uk
www.simplyscripts.com
www.script-o-rama.com
www.dailyscript.com
www.scriptcity.com
www.thescriptsource.net
```

There are also script books that feature a compilation of a particular show's episodes. Shows that have released script books include *Babylon 5*, *Buffy the Vampire Slayer*, *Doctor Who*, *Star Trek: The Next Generation*, *The West Wing*.

Some writers and production companies sometimes also publish scripts on their websites.

There is no harm in asking agents, writers, producers or the shows themselves if you can look at copy of their scripts. Below is a suggested list of shows you should watch and/or whose scripts you should read. Read as many scripts for as many shows as you can. In particular, look at the very first episode of the shows because that is in effect what you are writing.

UK	
Doctor Who	*Occupation*
Downton Abbey	*Scott & Bailey*
Hustle	*Sherlock*
Life on Mars	*Spooks*
Luther	*State of Play*
Mad Dogs	*The Hour*
Monroe	*The Street*
New Tricks	*Unforgiven*

US

Battlestar Galactica	*Once Upon A Time*
Blue Bloods	*The Good Wife*
Dexter	*The West Wing*
House	*The Wire*
Mad Men	

Script consultants

There are number of script consultant services on both sides of the Atlantic who will offer feedback on your script. Always check their credentials and understand the kind of coverage they will provide for your script. Below is a small list of consultants who provide feedback services. There are many others, so do your homework.

www.scriptangel.co.uk
www.bang2write.com
www.scriptshark.com
www.scriptpipeline.com
www.scriptapaloozatv.com
www.rocliffe.co.uk
www.script-consultant.co.uk
www.screenwritinggoldmine.com
www.industrialscripts.co.uk

Books

Lawrence Meyers (ed.), *Inside the TV Writer's Room* (Syracuse University Press)

Paul Ashton, *The Calling Card Script* (A&C Black)

J. Michael Straczynski, *The Complete Book of Scriptwriting* (Titan Books)

Eileen Quinn and Judy Counihan, *The Pitch* (Faber & Faber)

Russell T Davies and Benjamin Cook, *The Writer's Tale* (BBC Books)

Pamela Douglas, *Writing the TV Drama Series* (Michael Wiese Productions)

Glossary

Television drama, like everything else, has developed its own vocabulary. Below is a basic glossary to help you understand some of the terms of scriptwriting.

Act An act is composed of a number of scenes which culminate in a cliffhanger that usually leads into an advertising break on commercial television or an imaginary ad break on public and cable television. There may be between three and six acts in an episode.

Action/description This depicts on-screen events and conveys all non-dialogue information within a scene.

Agent This is someone who represents a writer. Most producers and broadcasters will deal only with a writer who has an agent.

Antagonist The rival of your hero.

Arc The journey a character takes that sees them undergo a change in circumstances and/or attitude.

Backstory The biography of your character that made them who they are by the time we meet them on screen for the first time.

Beat (1) A scene or step of a story.

Beat (2) A pause in the dialogue or action.

Breaking a story Establishing the significant turning points and act breaks in a story. This is a step taken before writing an outline.

Cliffhanger End-of-act moment of suspense, jeopardy or revelation that raises the stakes.

Development The process of taking a script from idea to production to make it the best it can be.

Dialogue Everything characters say.

Episode One part of a TV series or serial.

Executive producer The person responsible for the creative and business aspects of a show.

EXT. (Exterior) Used in the scene heading to signify an outside scene.

Greenlight Where a script or series is approved to go into production.

Hook The early moment that grabs an audience (or reader).

INT. (Interior) Used in the scene heading to signify an inside scene.

Logline One- (or two-) sentence summary of the story.

Outline A brief narrative story of your script or a 'scene-by-scene' in order where each scene has its own logline.

Pilot Usually the first episode of a proposed series – effectively a test episode.

Pitch Selling your story to a potential agent, producer or broadcaster.

Plot The structure of a story from start to finish.

Plot point A turning point or cliffhanger in your story.

Premise The situation created by your inciting incident – the *what if* ?

Producer The person responsible for the production process.

Protagonist The hero/heroine.

Rewrite Where a script is redrafted following pre-production and in response to production notes.

Scene Smallest dramatic unit that make up an act.

Scene heading The heading in the script that establishes where and when the scene takes place. Also known as: slug line.

Season A complete series of a show aired in a television year.

Serial A show where the characters evolve over the run of the episodes in a complete story.

Series A show that has a self-contained story about the regular characters.

Shooting script   The final draft of the script that goes into production.

Showrunner Usually the creator of the show who is ranked as an executive producer and who oversees the creative direction of the show.

Spec script   A script written with the hope of demonstrating the writer's ability with a view to getting an assignment on another show or, more rarely, in the hope of getting it made.

Staff writer   Writer employed on a high-volume episode show to write and/or contribute to the creative process of the show.

Storyline A synopsis of a story strand within an episode or over a number of episodes.

Syndication Minimum of 88 episodes that leads to a series being sold as a package to other stations or overseas markets.

Synopsis A brief outline of a story.

Teaser The drama before the opening credits which provides the hook to entice the audience. Also known as: cold opening.

Treatment The complete episode written in detail in prose form.

Working title The title of a show used for reference but probably not the one that will finally be used.

Index